Enjoy

Slow Cooker

Enjoy
Slow Cooker

This edition published in 2012
LOVE FOOD is an imprint of Parragon Books Ltd

Parragon
Queen Street House
4 Queen Street
Bath BA1 1HE, UK

ISBN: 978-1-4454-6769-6

Printed in China

Notes for the Reader
This book uses both metric and imperial measurements. Follow the same units of
measurement throughout; do not mix metric and imperial. All spoon measurements are
level: teaspoons are assumed to be 5 ml, and tablespoons are assumed to be 15 ml.
Unless otherwise stated, milk is assumed to be full fat, eggs and individual vegetables are
medium, and pepper is freshly ground black pepper.

The times given are an approximate guide only. Preparation times differ according to the
techniques used by different people and the cooking times may also vary from those
given. Optional ingredients, variations or serving suggestions have not been included in
the calculations.

Recipes using raw or very lightly cooked eggs should be avoided by infants, the elderly,
pregnant women, convalescents and anyone suffering from an illness. Pregnant and
breastfeeding women are advised to avoid eating peanuts and peanut products.
Sufferers from nut allergies should be aware that some of the ready-made ingredients
used in the recipes in this book may contain nuts. Always check the packaging before use.

contents

introduction

A slow cooker could revolutionize your everyday meals – it's a simple, tasty and economical way of cooking at a pace that suits busy lives. Join the thousands of people who have fallen in love with the convenient cooking style of the slow cooker and discover the versatility of this clever kitchen gadget. It's not just soups and stews, oh no! With a little preparation you can create a delicious one-pot dish that's full of flavour and packed with nutritious ingredients, and what's more, you can leave it to bubble away while you carry on with your day!

If you haven't yet joined the slow cooker revolution, where have you been? In the last few years, the humble slow cooker has seen a steady rise in popularity, and is now a well-loved (and well-used) instalment in kitchens the world over. As our day-to-day lives become ever busier, lots of us are having to change our domestic priorities and home-cooked meals are becoming a thing of the past. The slow cooker offers an easy, reliable solution. Simply prepare your ingredients, pop them in the pot and leave your delicious dish to cook, safe in the knowledge that dinner will be done by the time you return home.

A slow cooker operates at a much lower temperature than your oven or hob, and seals in all the juices often lost in traditional cooking processes. As a result, the slow cooker offers a long, gentle cooking time and produces tasty, nutritious meals, all with a minimum amount of hassle. It's an easy and (perhaps more importantly) cost-effective way to create great food for you and your family. Your slow cooker can be left for up to 12 hours while you get on with your life – food can't burn or dry up in your absence and when you're ready to eat all you have to do is serve. Better still, there's only one pot to wash up afterwards!

top tips

- It may be boring, but be sensible and read the manufacturer's instructions before you use your slow cooker for the first time, and keep them for future reference. The principles in this book are of course standardised, but familiarise yourself with your model and adjust your cooking methods accordingly.

- Your slow cooker is the perfect vessel for cooking cheaper cuts of meats in tasty stews and casseroles – the long, gentle cooking process is great for tenderising tougher meat and it's a great money saver!

- Always position your slow cooker on a flat, stable surface, well out of reach of children. For safety, ensure that the electric cable is tucked out of the way, too.

- Make sure that frozen food is thoroughly defrosted before adding it to the slow cooker.

- Remove the inner cooking pot (if your slow cooker has one) before adding prepared ingredients and wipe it clean before returning to the cooker base. This will keep your slow cooker in tip-top condition.

- Remember that your slow cooker works best when it is at least half full, but should never be more than two-thirds full. Always allow room for the ingredients to expand as they cook.

- Root vegetables take a long time to cook through, so always dice/slice finely if you're planning on cooking the dish for the minimum required time, and make sure they are completely covered in liquid.

- Resist the temptation to open the lid of the slow cooker, especially during the first half of the cooking time – it breaks the condensation seal, will reduce the temperature and as a result could take up to 20 minutes to return to its original heat.

- If you're leaving the slow cooker unattended, even if only for a short period of time, remember to turn the control down to low.

- Switch off and unplug the slow cooker before removing the inner cooking dish, or serving. Remember to wear oven gloves if you need to handle the heated inner part of the slow cooker – it gets very hot!

- If you are preparing something in the slow cooker that you intend to serve cold, remember to remove the dish from the slow cooker to cool. Place the food in a plastic container and store in the refrigerator once it has reached room temperature.

- Take care when removing the lid of the slow cooker as escaping steam may scald you. Never place the lid of the slow cooker on a hot surface, or into cold water when in use. Instead, place it on a chopping board or heat-proof mat and leave to cool.

- Allow your slow cooker to cool completely before washing it in hot water and dry thoroughly before returning to the base and putting away. Do not immerse the base in water – if it needs cleaning simply wipe the surface over with a damp cloth and leave to dry.

- Never use the slow cooker to heat prepared dishes, or reheat leftovers. It simply doesn't heat the food hot enough, quickly enough to get rid of bacteria.

- If you are using dried beans, always soak them in fresh water for at least 5 hours. Drain and rinse the beans, then cover with fresh water and bring to the boil in a saucepan. Boil rapidly for at least 10 minutes, drain and rinse again before adding to the slow cooker.

- Browning meat and some poultry before adding it to the slow cooker is really important for adding flavour to your dishes. It might seem like an unnecessary step, but the extra few minutes spent preparing your ingredients will be apparent come dinner time!

beef stock

makes 1.7 litres/3 pints
- 1 kg/2 lb 4 oz beef marrow bones, sawn into 7.5-cm/3-inch pieces
- 650 g/1 lb 7 oz stewing beef in a single piece
- 2.8 litres/5 pints water
- 4 cloves
- 2 onions, halved
- 2 celery sticks, roughly chopped
- 8 peppercorns
- 1 bouquet garni

1 Put the bones in a large saucepan and put the stewing beef on top. Pour in the water and bring to the boil over a low heat. Skim off the scum that rises to the surface.

2 Press a clove into each onion half and add to the pan with the celery, peppercorns and bouquet garni. Partially cover and simmer gently for 3 hours. Remove the stewing beef from the pan, partially re-cover and simmer for a further hour.

3 Remove the pan from the heat and leave to cool. Strain the stock into a bowl, cover with clingfilm and chill in the refrigerator for at least 1 hour and preferably overnight.

4 Remove and discard the layer of fat that has set on the surface. Use immediately or freeze for up to 6 months.

chicken stock

makes 2.5 litres/4½ pints
- 1.3 kg/3 lb chicken wings and necks
- 2 onions, cut into wedges
- 4 litres/7 pints water
- 2 carrots, roughly chopped
- 2 celery sticks, roughly chopped
- 10 fresh parsley sprigs
- 4 fresh thyme sprigs
- 2 bay leaves
- 10 black peppercorns

1 Place the chicken and onions in a large saucepan and cook over a low heat, stirring frequently, until browned all over.

2 Pour in the water and stir well, scraping up any sediment from the base of the pan. Bring to the boil.

3 Add the remaining ingredients, partially cover the pan and simmer gently, stirring occasionally, for 3 hours.

4 Remove the pan from the heat and leave to cool. Strain the stock into a bowl, cover with clingfilm and chill in the refrigerator for at least 1 hour and preferably overnight.

5 Remove and discard the layer of fat that has set on the surface. Use immediately or freeze for up to 6 months.

fish stock

makes 1.3 litres/2¼ pints

- 650 g/1 lb 7 oz white fish heads, bones and trimmings
- 1 onion, roughly chopped
- 2 celery sticks, roughly chopped
- 1 carrot, roughly chopped
- 1 bay leaf
- 4 fresh parsley sprigs
- 4 black peppercorns
- ½ lemon, sliced
- 125 ml/4 fl oz dry white wine
- 1.3 litres/2¼ pints water

1 Cut out and discard the gills from the fish heads, then rinse the heads, bones and trimmings. Place them in a large saucepan

2 Add the remaining ingredients. Bring to the boil and skim off the scum that rises to the surface. Lower the heat, partially cover and simmer gently for 25 minutes.

3 Remove the pan from the heat and leave to cool. Strain the stock into a bowl, without pressing down on the contents of the colander. Use immediately or freeze for up to 3 months.

vegetable stock

makes 2 litres/3½ pints

- 2 tbsp sunflower or corn oil
- 115 g/4 oz onions, roughly chopped
- 115 g/4 oz leeks, roughly chopped
- 115 g/4 oz carrots, roughly chopped
- 4 celery sticks, roughly chopped
- 85 g/3 oz fennel, roughly chopped
- 85 g/3 oz tomatoes, roughly chopped
- 2.25 litres/4 pints water
- 1 bouquet garni

1 Heat the oil in a large saucepan. Add the onions and leeks and cook over a low heat, stirring occasionally, for 5 minutes, until softened.

2 Add the carrots, celery, fennel and tomatoes, cover and cook, stirring occasionally, for 10 minutes. Pour in the water, add the bouquet garni and bring to the boil. Lower the heat and simmer for 20 minutes.

3 Remove the pan from the heat and leave to cool. Strain the stock into a bowl. Use immediately or freeze for up to 3 months.

Enjoy
light-bites & lunches

tomato & lentil soup

serves 4

- 2 tbsp sunflower oil
- 1 onion, chopped
- 1 garlic clove, finely chopped
- 2 celery sticks, roughly chopped
- 2 carrots, roughly chopped
- 1 tsp ground cumin
- 1 tsp ground coriander
- 175 g/6 oz red or yellow lentils
- 1 tbsp tomato purée
- 1.2 litres/2 pints vegetable stock
- 400 g/14 oz canned chopped tomatoes
- 1 bay leaf
- salt and pepper
- crème fraîche and toasted crusty bread, to serve

1 Heat the oil in a saucepan. Add the onion and garlic and cook over a low heat, stirring occasionally, for 5 minutes, until softened. Stir in the celery and carrots and cook, stirring occasionally, for a further 4 minutes. Stir in the ground cumin and coriander and cook for 1 minute, then add the lentils.

2 Mix the tomato purée with a little of the stock in a small bowl and add to the pan with the remaining stock, the tomatoes and bay leaf. Bring to the boil, then transfer to the slow cooker. Stir well, cover and cook on low for 3½–4 hours.

3 Remove and discard the bay leaf. Transfer the soup to a food processor or blender and process until smooth. Season to taste with salt and pepper. Ladle into warmed soup bowls, top each with a swirl of crème fraîche and serve immediately with toasted crusty bread.

new england clam chowder

serves 4

- 25 g/1 oz butter
- 1 onion, finely chopped
- 2 potatoes, peeled and cut into cubes
- 1 large carrot, diced
- 400 ml/14 fl oz fish stock or water
- 280 g/10 oz canned clams, drained
- 250 ml/9 fl oz double cream
- salt and pepper
- chopped fresh parsley, to garnish
- crusty bread, to serve

1 Melt the butter in a frying pan, add the onion and fry over a medium heat for 4–5 minutes, stirring, until golden.

2 Transfer the onion to the slow cooker with the potatoes, carrot, stock and salt and pepper. Cover and cook on high for 3 hours.

3 Add the clams and the cream to the slow cooker and stir to mix evenly. Cover and cook for a further 1 hour.

4 Adjust the seasoning to taste. Transfer to warmed serving bowls, sprinkle with parsley and serve immediately with crusty bread.

salmon chowder

serves 4
- 15 g/½ oz butter
- 1 tbsp sunflower oil
- 1 onion, finely chopped
- 1 leek, finely chopped
- 1 fennel bulb, finely chopped, feathery tops reserved
- 280 g/10 oz potatoes, diced
- 700 ml/1¼ pints fish stock
- 450 g/1 lb salmon fillet, skinned and cut into cubes
- 300 ml/10 fl oz milk
- 150 ml/5 fl oz single cream
- 2 tbsp chopped fresh dill
- salt and pepper

1 Melt the butter with the oil in a saucepan. Add the onion, leek and fennel and cook over a low heat, stirring occasionally, for 5 minutes. Add the potatoes and cook, stirring occasionally, for a further 4 minutes, then pour in the stock and season to taste with salt and pepper. Bring to the boil, then transfer to the slow cooker. Cover and cook on low for 3 hours, until the potatoes are tender.

2 Meanwhile, chop the fennel fronds and set aside. Add the salmon to the slow cooker, pour in the milk and stir gently. Re-cover and cook on low for 30 minutes, until the fish flakes easily.

3 Gently stir in the cream, dill and the reserved fennel fronds, re-cover and cook for a further 10–15 minutes, until heated through. Taste and adjust the seasoning, adding salt and pepper if needed. Serve immediately.

chicken noodle soup

serves 4

- 1 onion, diced
- 2 celery sticks, diced
- 2 carrots, diced
- 1 kg/2 lb 4 oz oven-ready chicken
- 700 ml/1¼ pints hot chicken stock
- 115 g/4 oz dried egg tagliatelle
- salt and pepper
- 2 tbsp chopped fresh dill, to garnish

1 Place the onion, celery and carrots in the slow cooker. Season the chicken all over with salt and pepper and place on top. Pour the stock over. Cover and cook on low for 5 hours.

2 Leaving the juices in the slow cooker, carefully lift out the chicken and remove the meat from the carcass, discarding the bones and skin. Cut the meat into bite-sized pieces.

3 Skim the excess fat from the juices, then return the chicken to the slow cooker. Turn the setting to high.

4 Bring a large saucepan of lightly salted water to the boil. Add the pasta, bring back to the boil and cook for 8–10 minutes, or until tender but still firm to the bite. Drain, add to the chicken and stir well.

5 Ladle into warmed soup bowls and garnish with dill. Serve immediately.

barbecue chicken

serves 4

- 8 skinless chicken drumsticks or thighs
- 3 tbsp tomato purée
- 2 tbsp clear honey
- 1 tbsp Worcestershire sauce
- juice of ½ lemon
- ½ tsp crushed dried chillies
- 1 garlic clove, crushed
- salt and pepper

1 Using a sharp knife, cut slashes into the thickest parts of the chicken flesh.

2 Mix the tomato purée, honey, Worcestershire sauce, lemon juice, chillies and garlic together and season with salt and pepper. Add the chicken and toss well to coat evenly.

3 Arrange the chicken in the slow cooker, cover and cook on high for 3 hours.

4 Remove the chicken with a slotted spoon and transfer to a warmed serving dish. Spoon the juices over the chicken, skimming off any fat. Serve immediately.

chicken quesadillas

serves 4

- 4 skinless chicken breast fillets
- ½ tsp crushed dried chillies
- 2 cloves garlic, crushed
- 2 tbsp finely chopped parsley
- 2 tbsp olive oil
- 350 g/12 oz cherry tomatoes
- 4 large wheat tortillas
- 250 g/9 oz mozzarella cheese
- salt and pepper

1 Place the chicken in a bowl with the chillies, garlic, parsley and 1 tablespoon of oil, and turn to coat evenly. Cover and leave in the refrigerator to marinate for at least 1 hour, or overnight.

2 Tip the tomatoes into the slow cooker and arrange the chicken breasts on top. Season with salt and pepper. Cover and cook on high for 2 hours, until tender.

3 Remove the chicken and shred the meat using two forks. Place on one side of each tortilla and top with the tomatoes. Chop or tear the mozzarella and arrange on top. Moisten the edges of the tortillas and fold over to enclose the filling.

4 Brush a griddle or large frying pan with the remaining oil and place over a medium heat. Add the quesadillas to the pan and cook until golden, turning once. Cut into wedges and serve. Any spare juices can be spooned over.

chipotle chicken

serves 4

- 4–6 dried chipotle chillies
- 4 garlic cloves, unpeeled
- 1 small onion, finely chopped
- 400 g/14 oz canned chopped tomatoes
- 300 ml/10 fl oz hot chicken or vegetable stock
- 4 skinless chicken breasts
- salt and pepper
- chopped fresh coriander, to garnish

1 Preheat the oven to 200°C/400°F/Gas Mark 6. Place the chillies in a bowl and pour in just enough hot water to cover. Set aside to soak for 30 minutes. Meanwhile, place the unpeeled garlic cloves on a baking sheet and roast in the preheated oven for about 10 minutes, until soft. Remove from the oven and set aside to cool.

2 Drain the chillies, reserving 125 ml/4 fl oz of the soaking water. Deseed the chillies, if you like, and chop roughly. Place the chillies and reserved soaking water in a blender or food processor and process to a purée. Peel and mash the garlic in a bowl.

3 Place the chilli purée, garlic, onion and tomatoes in the slow cooker and stir in the stock. Season the chicken with salt and pepper to taste and place in the slow cooker. Cover and cook on low for about 5 hours, until the chicken is tender and cooked through.

4 Lift the chicken out of the slow cooker with a slotted spoon, cover and keep warm. Pour the cooking liquid into a saucepan and bring to the boil on the hob. Boil for 5–10 minutes, until reduced. Transfer the chicken to warmed serving plates and pour the sauce over the chicken. Serve immediately garnished with coriander.

sweet & sour chicken wings

serves 4–6

- 1 kg/2 lb 4 oz chicken wings, tips removed
- 2 celery sticks, chopped
- 700 ml/1¼ pints hot chicken stock
- 2 tbsp cornflour
- 3 tbsp white wine vinegar or rice vinegar
- 3 tbsp dark soy sauce
- 5 tbsp sweet chilli sauce
- 55 g/2 oz soft light brown sugar
- 400 g/14 oz canned pineapple chunks in juice, drained
- 200 g/7 oz canned sliced bamboo shoots, drained and rinsed
- ½ green pepper, deseeded and thinly sliced
- ½ red pepper, deseeded and thinly sliced
- salt
- steamed pak choi, to serve

1 Put the chicken wings and celery in the slow cooker and season well with salt. Pour in the stock, cover and cook on low for 5 hours.

2 Drain the chicken wings, reserving 350 ml/12 fl oz of the stock, and keep warm. Pour the reserved stock into a saucepan and stir in the cornflour. Add the vinegar, soy sauce and chilli sauce. Place over a medium heat and stir in the sugar. Cook, stirring constantly, for 5 minutes, or until the sugar has dissolved completely and the sauce is thickened, smooth and clear.

3 Reduce the heat, stir in the pineapple, bamboo shoots and peppers and simmer gently for 2–3 minutes. Stir in the chicken wings until they are thoroughly coated, then transfer to warmed serving bowls. Serve immediately with pak choi.

spicy pulled pork

serves 4

- 2 onions, sliced
- 1.5 kg/3 lb 5 oz boned and rolled pork shoulder
- 2 tbsp demerara sugar
- 2 tbsp Worcestershire sauce
- 1 tbsp American mustard
- 2 tbsp tomato ketchup
- 1 tbsp cider vinegar
- salt and pepper
- burger buns or ciabatta rolls, to serve

1 Put the onions in the slow cooker and place the pork on top. Mix the sugar, Worcestershire sauce, mustard, ketchup and vinegar together and spread all over the surface of the pork. Season to taste with salt and pepper. Cover and cook on low for 8 hours.

2 Remove the pork from the slow cooker and use two forks to pull it apart into shreds.

3 Skim any excess fat from the juices and stir a little juice into the pork. Serve in burger buns, with the remaining juices for spooning over.

maple-glazed pork ribs

serves 4

- 1 onion, finely chopped
- 2 plum tomatoes, diced
- 3 tbsp maple syrup
- 2 tbsp soy sauce
- 2 tsp hot chilli sauce
- 1.5 kg/3 lb 5 oz meaty pork ribs, cut into single ribs
- salt and pepper

1 Combine the onion, tomatoes, maple syrup, soy sauce, chilli sauce and salt and pepper to taste in a large bowl. Add the pork ribs and turn to coat evenly.

2 Arrange the ribs in the slow cooker, cover and cook on high for 4 hours. If possible, turn the ribs halfway through the cooking time.

3 Lift out the ribs and place on a warmed platter. Skim the excess fat from the juices and spoon the juices over the ribs to serve.

bouillabaisse

serves 6

- 2.25 kg/5 lb mixed white fish, such as red mullet, sea bream, sea bass, monkfish and whiting, filleted and bones and heads reserved, if possible
- 450 g/1 lb raw prawns
- grated rind of 1 orange
- pinch of saffron threads
- 4 garlic cloves, finely chopped
- 225 ml/8 fl oz olive oil
- 2 onions, finely chopped
- 1 leek, thinly sliced
- 4 potatoes, thinly sliced
- 2 large tomatoes, peeled and chopped
- 1 bunch fresh flat-leaf parsley, chopped
- 1 fresh fennel sprig
- 1 fresh thyme sprig
- 1 bay leaf
- 2 cloves
- 6 black peppercorns
- 1 strip thinly pared orange rind
- sea salt
- lightly toasted crusty bread, to serve

1 Cut the fish fillets into bite-sized pieces. Peel and devein the prawns, reserving the heads and shells. Rinse the fish bones, if using, and cut away the gills from the fish heads. Place the chunks of fish and the prawns in a large bowl. Sprinkle with the grated orange rind, saffron, half the garlic and 2 tablespoons of the oil. Cover and set aside in the refrigerator.

2 Put the remaining garlic, the onions, leek, potatoes, tomatoes, parsley, fennel, thyme, bay leaf, cloves, peppercorns and strip of orange rind into the slow cooker. Add the fish heads and bones, if using, and the prawn shells and heads. Pour in the remaining oil and enough boiling water to cover the ingredients by 2.5 cm/1 inch. Season to taste with sea salt. Cover and cook on low for 8 hours.

3 Strain the stock and return the liquid to the slow cooker. Discard the flavourings, fish and prawn trimmings and the bay leaf but reserve the vegetables and return them to the slow cooker if you like. Add the fish and prawn mixture, re-cover and cook on high for 30 minutes, until the fish is cooked through and flakes easily.

4 Ladle into warmed bowls and serve immediately with toasted crusty bread.

tagliatelle with tuna

serves 4

- 200 g/7 oz dried egg tagliatelle
- 400 g/14 oz canned tuna in oil, drained
- 1 bunch spring onions, sliced
- 175 g/6 oz frozen peas
- 2 tsp hot chilli sauce
- 600 ml/1 pint hot chicken stock
- 115 g/4 oz grated Cheddar cheese
- salt and pepper

1 Bring a large saucepan of lightly salted water to the boil. Add the pasta, return to the boil and cook for 2 minutes, until the pasta ribbons are loose. Drain.

2 Break up the tuna into bite-sized chunks and place in the slow cooker with the pasta, spring onions and peas. Season to taste with salt and pepper.

3 Add the chilli sauce to the stock and pour over the ingredients in the slow cooker. Sprinkle the grated cheese over the top. Cover and cook on low for 2 hours. Serve immediately on warmed plates.

beef & chipotle burritos

serves 4

- 1 tbsp olive oil
- 1 onion, sliced
- 600 g/1 lb 5 oz beef chuck steak
- 1 dried chipotle pepper, soaked in boiling water for 20 minutes
- 1 garlic clove, crushed
- 1 tsp ground cumin
- 400 g/14 oz canned chopped tomatoes
- 8 tortillas
- salt and pepper
- soured cream and green salad, to serve

1 Heat the oil in a frying pan and fry the onion for 3–4 minutes, until golden. Tip into the slow cooker and arrange the beef on top. Drain and chop the chipotle. Sprinkle over the meat with the garlic, cumin, tomatoes and salt and pepper.

2 Cover and cook on low for 4 hours, until the meat is tender.

3 Warm the tortillas. Remove the beef from the slow cooker and shred with a fork. Divide between the tortillas and spoon over the sauce. Wrap and serve with soured cream and green salad.

pork & beans

serves 4

- 2 tbsp sunflower oil
- 4 pork chops, trimmed of excess fat
- 1 onion, chopped
- 400 g / 14 oz canned chopped tomatoes
- 425 g / 15 oz canned baked beans
- butter, for greasing, plus extra for browning (optional)
- 700 g / 1 lb 9 oz potatoes, thinly sliced
- 425 ml / 15 fl oz hot chicken stock
- salt and pepper

1 Heat the oil in a frying pan. Season the chops well with salt and pepper, add to the pan and cook over a medium heat for 2–3 minutes on each side, until evenly browned. Remove the pan from the heat and transfer the chops to a plate.

2 Mix the onion, tomatoes and beans together in a bowl and season to taste with salt and pepper.

3 Lightly grease the slow cooker pot with butter, then make a layer of half the potatoes in the base. Cover with half the tomato and bean mixture. Put the chops on top, then add the remaining tomato and bean mixture. Cover with the remaining potato slices.

4 Pour in the stock, cover and cook on low for 8–10 hours. If wished, remove the lid, dot the topping with butter and place the slow cooker pot under a preheated grill to brown the potatoes before serving.

cured ham cooked in cider

serves 6

- 1 kg/2 lb 4 oz boneless gammon joint
- 1 onion, halved
- 4 cloves
- 6 black peppercorns
- 1 tsp juniper berries
- 1 celery stick, roughly chopped
- 1 carrot, sliced
- 1 litre/1¾ pints medium cider
- salad, to serve

1 Place the gammon in the slow cooker. Stud each onion half with two of the cloves and add to the slow cooker with the peppercorns, juniper berries, celery and carrot.

2 Pour in the cider, cover and cook on low for 8 hours, until the meat is tender.

3 Remove the gammon from the cooker and place on a board. Cover with foil and leave to stand for 10–15 minutes. Discard the cooking liquid and flavourings.

4 Cut off any rind and fat from the gammon joint and carve into slices. Transfer to serving plates and serve immediately with a salad.

tex-mex bean dip

serves 4

- 2 tbsp sunflower oil
- 1 onion, finely chopped
- 2 garlic cloves, finely chopped
- 2–3 fresh green chillies, deseeded and finely chopped
- 400 g/14 oz canned refried beans or red kidney beans
- 2 tbsp chilli sauce or taco sauce
- 6 tbsp hot vegetable stock
- 115 g/4 oz Cheddar cheese, grated
- salt and pepper
- 1 fresh red chilli, deseeded and shredded, to garnish
- tortilla chips, to serve

1 Heat the oil in a large, heavy-based frying pan. Add the onion, garlic and chillies and cook, stirring occasionally, over a low heat for 5 minutes, until the onion is soft and translucent. Transfer to the slow cooker.

2 Add the refried beans to the slow cooker. If using red kidney beans, drain well and rinse under cold running water. Reserve 2 tablespoons of the beans and mash the remainder coarsely with a potato masher. Add all the beans to the slow cooker.

3 Add the sauce, stock and cheese, season with salt and pepper and stir well. Cover and cook on low for 2 hours.

4 Transfer the dip to a serving bowl, garnish with shredded red chilli and serve warm with tortilla chips on the side.

warm chickpea salad

serves 6

- 225 g/8 oz dried chickpeas, soaked overnight, or for at least 5 hours
- 115 g/4 oz stoned black olives
- 4 spring onions, finely chopped
- fresh parsley sprigs, to garnish
- crusty bread, to serve

dressing

- 2 tbsp red wine vinegar
- 2 tbsp mixed chopped fresh herbs, such as parsley, rosemary and thyme
- 3 garlic cloves, very finely chopped
- 125 ml/4 fl oz extra virgin olive oil
- salt and pepper

1 Drain and rinse the chickpeas, place in a saucepan, cover with fresh cold water and bring to the boil. Boil rapidly for at least 10 minutes, then remove from the heat, drain and rinse again. Place the chickpeas in the slow cooker and add enough boiling water to cover. Cover and cook on low for 12 hours.

2 Drain well and transfer to a bowl. Stir in the olives and spring onions.

3 To make the dressing, whisk together the vinegar, herbs and garlic in a jug and season to taste with salt and pepper. Gradually whisk in the olive oil. Pour the dressing over the still-warm chickpeas and toss lightly to coat. Garnish with the parsley sprigs and serve warm with crusty bread.

stuffed peppers

serves 4

- 100 g/3½ oz basmati rice
- 4 red peppers
- 400 g/14 oz canned chickpeas, drained
- 100 g/3½ oz canned or frozen sweetcorn
- 4 spring onions, sliced
- 1 tbsp chopped fresh thyme
- 1 tbsp olive oil
- 150 ml/5 fl oz vegetable stock
- salt and pepper

1 Cook the rice in lightly salted, boiling water for 10 minutes, until almost tender. Drain well.

2 Slice the tops from the peppers and remove the seeds and membranes. Cut a small slice from the base of each so they sit firmly.

3 Mix the rice, chickpeas, sweetcorn, onions, thyme, oil and salt and pepper together. Spoon into the peppers and replace the lids.

4 Place the peppers in the slow cooker. Pour in the stock, cover and cook on low for 5 hours, until tender. Transfer to warmed serving plates and serve immediately.

cabbage roulades

serves 6

- 225 g/8 oz mixed nuts, finely ground
- 2 onions, finely chopped
- 1 garlic clove, finely chopped
- 2 celery sticks, finely chopped
- 115 g/4 oz Cheddar cheese, grated
- 1 tsp finely chopped fresh thyme
- 2 eggs
- 1 tsp yeast extract
- 12 large green cabbage leaves

tomato sauce

- 2 tbsp sunflower oil
- 2 onions, chopped
- 2 garlic cloves, finely chopped
- 600 g/1 lb 5 oz canned chopped tomatoes
- 2 tbsp tomato purée
- 1½ tsp sugar
- 1 bay leaf
- salt and pepper

1 To make the tomato sauce, heat the oil in a heavy-based saucepan. Add the onions and cook over a medium heat, stirring occasionally, for 5 minutes, until softened. Stir in the garlic and cook for 1 minute, then add the tomatoes, tomato purée, sugar and bay leaf. Season to taste with salt and pepper and bring to the boil. Reduce the heat and simmer gently for 20 minutes, until thickened.

2 Meanwhile, mix the nuts, onions, garlic, celery, cheese and thyme together in a bowl. Lightly beat the eggs with the yeast extract in a jug, then stir into the nut mixture. Set aside.

3 Cut out the thick stalk from the cabbage leaves. Blanch the leaves in a large saucepan of boiling water for 5 minutes, then drain and refresh under cold water. Pat dry with kitchen paper.

4 Place a little of the nut mixture on the stalk end of each cabbage leaf. Fold the sides over, then roll up to make a neat parcel. Repeat with the remaining cabbage leaves and nut mixture.

5 Arrange the parcels in the slow cooker, seam-side down. Remove and discard the bay leaf from the tomato sauce and pour the sauce over the cabbage rolls. Cover and cook on low for 3–4 hours. Serve the cabbage roulades hot or cold.

louisiana courgettes

serves 6

- 1 kg/2 lb 4 oz courgettes, thickly sliced
- 1 onion, finely chopped
- 2 garlic cloves, finely chopped
- 2 red peppers, deseeded and chopped
- 5 tbsp hot vegetable stock
- 4 tomatoes, peeled and chopped
- 25 g/1 oz butter, diced
- salt and cayenne pepper
- crusty bread rolls, to serve

1 Place the courgettes, onion, garlic and red peppers in the slow cooker and season to taste with salt and cayenne pepper. Pour in the stock and mix well.

2 Sprinkle the chopped tomatoes on top and dot with the butter. Cover and cook on high for 2½ hours, until tender. Serve immediately with crusty bread rolls.

aubergine timbales

serves 4

- 2 aubergines
- 3 tbsp olive oil, plus extra for greasing
- 2 onions, finely chopped
- 2 red peppers, deseeded and chopped
- 1 large tomato, peeled and chopped
- 6 tbsp milk
- 2 egg yolks
- pinch of ground cinnamon
- 85 g/3 oz crispbread, finely crushed
- salt and pepper
- fresh flat-leaf parsley sprigs, to garnish
- soured cream, to serve

1 Halve the aubergines and scoop out the flesh. Reserve the shells and dice the flesh. Heat the oil in a large frying pan. Add the onions and cook over a low heat, for 5 minutes. Add the diced aubergines, red peppers and tomato and cook for 15–20 minutes, until soft. Remove the pan from the heat.

2 Transfer the mixture to a food processor or blender and process to a purée. Beat the milk, egg yolks and cinnamon in a jug. Season with salt and pepper, then stir into the vegetable purée.

3 Brush four ramekins with oil and sprinkle with enough of the crispbread crumbs to coat. Tip out any excess. Mix about three quarters of the remaining crumbs into the vegetable purée. Slice the aubergine shells into strips and use them to line the ramekins, leaving the ends overlapping the rims. Spoon the filling into the ramekins, sprinkle with the remaining crumbs and fold over the overlapping ends of the aubergine. Cover the ramekins with foil.

4 Stand the ramekins on a trivet in the slow cooker and pour in enough boiling water to come about one third of the way up the sides of the ramekins. Cover and cook on high for 2 hours.

5 Lift the ramekins out of the slow cooker and remove the foil. Invert onto serving plates, garnish with parsley sprigs and serve immediately with soured cream.

mixed bean chilli

serves 4–6

- 115 g/4 oz dried red kidney beans, soaked overnight, or for at least 5 hours
- 115 g/4 oz dried black beans, soaked overnight, or for at least 5 hours
- 115 g/4 oz dried pinto beans, soaked overnight, or for at least 5 hours
- 2 tbsp corn oil
- 1 onion, chopped
- 1 garlic clove, finely chopped
- 1 fresh red chilli, deseeded and chopped
- 1 yellow pepper, deseeded and chopped
- 1 tsp ground cumin
- 1 tbsp chilli powder
- 1 litre/1¾ pints vegetable stock
- 1 tbsp sugar
- salt and pepper
- chopped fresh coriander, to garnish
- crusty bread, to serve

1 Drain and rinse the beans, place in a saucepan, cover with fresh cold water and bring to the boil. Boil rapidly for at least 10 minutes, then remove from the heat, drain and rinse again.

2 Heat the oil in a large heavy-based saucepan. Add the onion, garlic, chilli and yellow pepper and cook over a medium heat, stirring occasionally, for 5 minutes. Stir in the cumin and chilli powder and cook, stirring, for 1–2 minutes. Add the drained beans and stock and bring to the boil. Boil vigorously for 15 minutes.

3 Transfer the mixture to the slow cooker, cover and cook on low for 10 hours, until the beans are tender.

4 Season to taste with salt and pepper, then ladle about one third into a bowl. Mash well with a potato masher, then return the mashed beans to the slow cooker and stir in the sugar. Transfer to warmed serving bowls and garnish with chopped coriander. Serve immediately with crusty bread.

sweet & sour sicilian pasta

serves 4

- 4 tbsp olive oil
- 1 large red onion, sliced
- 2 garlic cloves, finely chopped
- 2 red peppers, deseeded and sliced
- 2 courgettes, cut into batons
- 1 aubergine, cut into batons
- 450 ml/16 fl oz passata
- 4 tbsp lemon juice
- 2 tbsp balsamic vinegar
- 55 g/2 oz stoned black olives, sliced
- 1 tbsp sugar
- 400 g/14 oz dried fettuccine
- salt and pepper
- fresh flat-leaf parsley sprigs, to garnish

1 Heat the oil in a large, heavy-based saucepan. Add the onion, garlic and peppers and cook over a low heat, stirring occasionally, for 5 minutes. Add the courgettes and aubergine and cook, stirring occasionally, for a further 5 minutes. Stir in the passata and 150 ml/5 fl oz of water and bring to the boil. Stir in the lemon juice, vinegar, olives and sugar and season with salt and pepper.

2 Transfer the mixture to the slow cooker. Cover and cook on low for 5 hours until all the vegetables are tender.

3 To cook the pasta, bring a large saucepan of lightly salted water to the boil. Add the fettuccine and bring back to the boil. Cook for 10–12 minutes until the pasta is tender but still firm to the bite. Drain and transfer to a warmed serving dish. Spoon the vegetable mixture over the pasta, toss lightly, garnish with parsley and serve.

winter vegetable medley

serves 4

- 2 tbsp sunflower oil
- 2 onions, peeled and chopped
- 3 carrots, sliced lengthways
- 3 parsnips, sliced lengthways
- 2 bunches celery, sliced lengthways
- 2 tbsp chopped fresh parsley
- 1 tbsp chopped fresh coriander
- 300 ml/10 fl oz vegetable stock
- salt and pepper

1 Heat the oil in a large, heavy-based saucepan. Add the onions and cook over a medium heat, stirring occasionally, for 5 minutes, until softened. Add the carrots, parsnips and celery and cook, stirring occasionally, for a further 5 minutes. Stir in the herbs, season with salt and pepper and pour in the stock. Bring to the boil.

2 Transfer the vegetable mixture to the slow cooker, cover and cook on high for 3 hours, until tender. Taste and adjust the seasoning if necessary. Using a slotted spoon, transfer the medley to warmed plates, then spoon over a little of the cooking liquid. Serve immediately.

risotto with spring vegetables

serves 4

- 1.2 litres/2 pints vegetable stock
- large pinch of saffron threads
- 55 g/2 oz butter
- 1 tbsp olive oil
- 1 onion, chopped
- 2 garlic cloves, finely chopped
- 225 g/8 oz risotto rice
- 3 tbsp dry white wine
- 1 bay leaf
- 250 g/9 oz mixed spring vegetables, such as asparagus spears, French beans, baby carrots, baby broad beans and petits pois, thawed if frozen
- 2 tbsp chopped flat-leaf parsley
- 55 g/2 oz Parmesan cheese, grated
- salt and pepper

1 Put 6 tablespoons of the stock into a small bowl, crumble in the saffron threads and leave to infuse. Reserve 150 ml/5 fl oz of the remaining stock and heat the remainder in a saucepan.

2 Meanwhile, melt half of the butter with the oil in a separate large saucepan. Add the onion and garlic and cook over a low heat for 5 minutes, until softened. Stir in the rice and cook, stirring constantly, for 1–2 minutes, until all the grains are coated. Pour in the wine and cook, stirring constantly, for a few minutes, until all the alcohol has evaporated. Season to taste with salt and pepper. Pour in the hot stock and the saffron mixture, add the bay leaf and bring to the boil, stirring constantly.

3 Transfer the mixture to the slow cooker, cover and cook on low for 2 hours. Meanwhile, if using fresh vegetables, blanch in boiling water for 5 minutes. Drain and reserve. Stir the reserved stock into the rice mixture, if it seems dry, and add the mixed vegetables, sprinkling them evenly over the top. Re-cover and cook on low for a further 30–45 minutes, until heated through. Remove and discard the bay leaf. Gently stir in the parsley, the remaining butter and the cheese and serve immediately.

Enjoy
everyday
eats

traditional pot roast

serves 6

- 1 onion, finely chopped
- 4 carrots, sliced
- 4 baby turnips, sliced
- 4 celery sticks, sliced
- 2 potatoes, sliced
- 1 sweet potato, sliced
- 1.3–1.8 kg/3–4 lb topside of beef, in one piece
- 1 bouquet garni
- 300 ml/10 fl oz hot beef stock
- salt and pepper

1 Place the onion, carrots, turnips, celery, potatoes and sweet potato in the slow cooker and stir to mix well.

2 Rub the beef all over with salt and pepper, then place on top of the bed of vegetables. Add the bouquet garni and pour in the stock. Cover and cook on low for 9–10 hours, until the beef is cooked to your liking. Remove the bouquet garni and serve immediately.

chunky beef chilli

serves 4

- 250 g/9 oz dried red kidney beans, soaked overnight, or for at least 5 hours
- 600 ml/1 pint cold water
- 2 garlic cloves, chopped
- 5 tbsp tomato purée
- 1 small green chilli, chopped
- 2 tsp ground cumin
- 2 tsp ground coriander
- 600 g/1 lb 5 oz chuck steak, diced
- 1 large onion, chopped
- 1 large green pepper, deseeded and sliced
- salt and pepper
- soured cream, to serve

1 Drain and rinse the kidney beans, place in a saucepan, cover with fresh cold water and bring to the boil. Boil rapidly for at least 10 minutes, then remove from the heat, drain and rinse again. Place the beans in the slow cooker and add the 600 ml of cold water.

2 Mix the garlic, tomato purée, chilli, cumin and coriander together in a large bowl. Add the steak, onion and green pepper and mix to coat evenly.

3 Place the meat and vegetables on top of the beans, cover and cook on low for 9 hours, until the beans and meat are tender. Stir and season to taste with salt and pepper.

4 Transfer to warmed serving bowls and top with a swirl of soured cream. Serve immediately.

beef ragù with tagliatelle

serves 6

- 3 tbsp olive oil
- 85 g/3 oz pancetta or bacon, diced
- 1 onion, chopped
- 1 garlic clove, finely chopped
- 1 carrot, chopped
- 1 celery stick, chopped
- 450 g/1 lb minced steak
- 125 ml/4 fl oz red wine
- 2 tbsp tomato purée
- 400 g/14 oz canned chopped tomatoes
- 300 ml/10 fl oz beef stock
- ½ tsp dried oregano
- 1 bay leaf
- 450 g/1 lb dried tagliatelle
- salt and pepper
- grated Parmesan cheese, to serve

1 Heat the oil in a saucepan. Add the pancetta and cook over a medium heat, stirring frequently, for 3 minutes. Reduce the heat, add the onion, garlic, carrot and celery and cook, stirring occasionally, for 5 minutes, until the vegetables have softened.

2 Increase the heat to medium and add the minced steak. Cook, stirring frequently and breaking it up with a wooden spoon, for 8–10 minutes, until evenly browned. Pour in the wine and cook for a few minutes, until the alcohol has evaporated. Stir in the tomato purée, tomatoes, stock, oregano and bay leaf and season to taste with salt and pepper.

3 Bring to the boil, then transfer the ragù to the slow cooker. Cover and cook on low for 8–8½ hours.

4 Shortly before serving, bring a large saucepan of lightly salted water to the boil. Add the pasta, bring back to the boil and cook for 8–10 minutes, until tender but still firm to the bite. Drain and tip into a warmed serving bowl. Remove and discard the bay leaf, then add the ragù to the pasta. Toss with two forks, sprinkle with the Parmesan cheese and serve immediately.

beef stew

serves 6

- 4 tbsp plain flour
- 1 kg/2 lb 4 oz braising steak, cut into 4-cm/1½-inch cubes
- 2 tbsp sunflower oil
- 85 g/3 oz bacon, diced
- 55 g/2 oz butter
- 2 onions, thinly sliced
- 4 carrots, sliced
- 600 g/1 lb 5 oz potatoes, cut into chunks
- 115 g/4 oz mushrooms, sliced
- 1 bay leaf
- 2 fresh thyme sprigs, finely chopped, plus extra sprigs to garnish
- 1 tbsp fresh parsley, finely chopped
- 400 g/14 oz canned chopped tomatoes
- 350 ml/12 fl oz beef stock
- salt and pepper

1 Put the flour into a plastic food bag and season to taste with salt and pepper. Add the steak cubes, in batches, hold the top securely and shake well to coat. Transfer the meat to a plate.

2 Heat the oil in a large frying pan. Add the bacon and cook over a low heat, stirring frequently, for 5 minutes. Add the steak cubes, increase the heat to medium and cook, stirring frequently, for 8–10 minutes, until evenly browned. Remove the meat with a slotted spoon and set aside on a plate.

3 Wipe out the pan with kitchen paper, then return to a low heat and melt the butter. Add the onions and cook, stirring occasionally, for 5 minutes, until softened. Add the carrots, potatoes and mushrooms and cook, stirring occasionally, for a further 5 minutes.

4 Season to taste with salt and pepper, add the bay leaf, chopped thyme, parsley and tomatoes and pour in the stock. Bring to the boil, stirring occasionally, then remove the pan from the heat and transfer the mixture to the slow cooker. Stir in the meat, cover and cook on low for 8–9 hours. Remove and discard the bay leaf. Garnish with thyme sprigs and serve immediately.

beef in beer

serves 4–6

- 4 tbsp sunflower oil
- 1 kg/2 lb 4 oz topside of beef, in one piece
- 1.5 kg/3 lb 5 oz red onions, thinly sliced
- 500 ml/18 fl oz beef stock
- 1½ tbsp plain flour
- 350 ml/12 fl oz beer
- 3 garlic cloves, chopped
- 1 strip thinly pared lemon rind
- 1 bay leaf
- 2 tbsp molasses
- salt and pepper
- fresh flat-leaf parsley sprigs, to garnish

1 Heat the oil in a large frying pan. Add the beef and cook over a medium–high heat, turning occasionally, for 5–8 minutes, until evenly browned. Transfer the beef to the slow cooker.

2 Reduce the heat to low and add the onions to the pan. Cook, stirring occasionally, for 5 minutes, until softened. Stir in 2 tablespoons of the stock, scraping up the sediment from the base of the pan, and cook until all the liquid has evaporated. Add another 2 tablespoons of the stock and continue to cook for a further 15 minutes, adding 2 tablespoons of the stock each time the previous addition has evaporated.

3 Stir in the flour and cook, stirring constantly, for 1 minute, then gradually stir in the remaining stock and the beer. Increase the heat to medium and bring to the boil, stirring constantly.

4 Stir in the garlic, lemon rind, bay leaf and molasses and season to taste with salt and pepper. Transfer the onion mixture to the slow cooker, cover and cook on low for 8–9 hours, until the beef is cooked to your liking. Serve immediately, garnished with parsley sprigs.

daube of lamb

serves 6

- 300 ml / 10 fl oz dry white wine
- 3 tbsp brandy
- 1 tbsp olive oil
- 1 fresh rosemary sprig
- 1 bay leaf
- 1 tbsp chopped fresh parsley
- 2 cloves
- 6 allspice berries
- 6 black peppercorns
- 1 strip thinly pared orange rind
- 4 shallots, sliced
- 2 carrots, sliced
- 2 garlic cloves, finely chopped
- 1.3 kg / 3 lb diced lamb
- 115 g / 4 oz plain flour
- 4 rashers bacon, cut into 2.5-cm / 1-inch strips
- 2 onions, chopped
- 500 ml / 18 fl oz beef stock
- salt and pepper
- crusty bread, to serve

1 Put the wine, brandy, oil, rosemary, bay leaf, parsley, cloves, allspice berries, peppercorns, orange rind, shallots, carrots, garlic and lamb into a large non-metallic bowl and mix well. Cover with clingfilm and leave to marinate overnight in the refrigerator.

2 Drain the lamb cubes, reserving the marinade. Pat the lamb dry with kitchen paper. Put the flour into a plastic food bag and season to taste with salt and pepper. Add the lamb cubes, in batches, hold the top securely and shake well to coat. Transfer the meat to a plate.

3 Cook the bacon in a large non-stick or heavy-based saucepan over a medium heat for 3 minutes. Add the onions, reduce the heat and cook, stirring occasionally, for 5 minutes, until softened. Add the lamb, increase the heat to medium and cook, stirring frequently, for 8–10 minutes, until evenly browned. Pour in the reserved marinade and the stock and bring to the boil, stirring occasionally.

4 Transfer the mixture to the slow cooker, cover and cook on low for 8–9 hours, until the meat is tender. Skim off any fat from the surface and remove and discard the rosemary, bay leaf and orange rind. Taste and adjust the seasoning if necessary. Transfer to warmed serving plates and serve immediately with crusty bread.

lamb with spring vegetables

serves 4-6

- 5 tbsp olive oil
- 6 shallots, chopped
- 1 garlic clove, chopped
- 2 celery sticks, chopped
- 2 tbsp plain flour
- 700 g/1 lb 9 oz boned leg or shoulder of lamb, cut into 2.5-cm/1-inch cubes
- 850 ml/1½ pints chicken stock
- 115 g/4 oz pearl barley, rinsed
- 225 g/8 oz small turnips, halved
- 225 g/8 oz baby carrots
- 225 g/8 oz frozen petits pois, thawed
- 225 g/8 oz frozen baby broad beans, thawed
- salt and pepper
- chopped fresh parsley, to garnish

1 Heat 3 tablespoons of the oil in large saucepan. Add the shallots, garlic and celery and cook over a low heat, stirring occasionally, for 8–10 minutes, until softened. Meanwhile, put the flour into a plastic food bag and season well with salt and pepper. Add the lamb cubes, in batches, hold the top securely and shake well to coat. Transfer the meat to a plate. Transfer the softened vegetables to the slow cooker. Add the remaining oil to the pan and heat. Add the lamb, in batches if necessary, increase the heat to medium and cook, stirring frequently, for 8–10 minutes, until evenly browned.

2 Return all the lamb to the pan. Gradually stir in the stock, scraping up the sediment from the base of the pan. Stir in the pearl barley, turnips and carrots, season to taste with salt and pepper and bring to the boil. Transfer the mixture to the slow cooker and stir well. Cover and cook on low for 8–10 hours, until the lamb is tender. Add the petits pois and broad beans to the slow cooker, sprinkling them evenly on top of the stew. Re-cover and cook on low for a further 30 minutes, until heated through. Stir well, then taste and adjust the seasoning, adding salt and pepper if needed. Garnish with parsley and serve immediately.

lamb shanks with olives

serves 4

- 1½ tbsp plain flour
- 4 lamb shanks
- 2 tbsp olive oil
- 1 onion, sliced
- 2 garlic cloves, finely chopped
- 2 tsp sweet paprika
- 400 g/14 oz canned chopped tomatoes
- 2 tbsp tomato purée
- 2 carrots, sliced
- 2 tsp sugar
- 225 ml/8 fl oz red wine
- 5-cm/2-inch cinnamon stick
- 2 fresh rosemary sprigs
- 115 g/4 oz stoned black olives
- 2 tbsp lemon juice
- 2 tbsp chopped fresh mint, plus extra leaves to garnish
- salt and pepper

1 Put the flour into a plastic food bag and season to taste with salt and pepper. Add the lamb shanks, hold the top securely and shake well to coat.

2 Heat the oil in a large heavy-based saucepan. Add the lamb shanks and cook over a medium heat, turning frequently, for 6–8 minutes, until evenly browned. Transfer to a plate and set aside.

3 Add the onion and garlic to the pan and cook, stirring frequently, for 5 minutes, until softened. Stir in the paprika and cook for 1 minute. Add the tomatoes, tomato purée, carrots, sugar, wine, cinnamon stick and rosemary and bring to the boil.

4 Transfer the mixture to the slow cooker and add the lamb shanks. Cover and cook on low for 8 hours, until the lamb is very tender.

5 Add the olives, lemon juice and chopped mint to the slow cooker. Re-cover and cook on high for 30 minutes. Remove and discard the rosemary and cinnamon stick. Transfer to warmed serving plates, garnish with mint leaves and serve immediately.

pork with apple & herbs

serves 6

- 2 tbsp plain flour
- 800 g/1 lb 12 oz boneless pork, cut into 2.5-cm/1-inch cubes
- 5 tbsp sunflower oil
- 1 large onion, chopped
- 2 garlic cloves, finely chopped
- 2 eating apples, cored and cut into wedges
- 300 ml/10 fl oz dry cider or apple juice
- 600 ml/1 pint chicken stock
- 2 bay leaves
- 2 fresh sage sprigs
- 1 fresh rosemary sprig
- salt and pepper
- 3 tbsp chopped fresh parsley, to garnish
- mashed potatoes, to serve

1 Put the flour into a plastic food bag and season to taste with salt and pepper. Add the pork cubes, in batches, hold the top securely and shake well to coat. Transfer the meat to a plate.

2 Heat 3 tablespoons of the oil in a large frying pan. Add the pork cubes, in batches if necessary, and cook over a medium heat, stirring frequently, for 5–8 minutes, until evenly browned. Transfer to a plate and set aside.

3 Add the remaining oil to the pan and heat. Add the onion and garlic and cook over a low heat, stirring occasionally, for 10 minutes, until softened and lightly browned. Add the apple wedges and cook, stirring occasionally, for 3–5 minutes, until beginning to colour. Gradually stir in the cider and stock, scraping up any sediment from the base of the pan, and bring to the boil. Season to taste with salt and pepper, add the bay leaves, sage and rosemary and transfer to the slow cooker. Stir in the pork, cover and cook on low for 6–7 hours.

4 Remove and discard the bay leaves and the sage and rosemary sprigs. Transfer the stew to warmed individual plates and sprinkle with the parsley. Serve immediately with mashed potatoes.

pork with peppers

serves 4

- 2 tbsp olive oil
- 4 pork chops, trimmed of excess fat
- 1 shallot, chopped
- 2 garlic cloves, finely chopped
- 2 orange peppers, deseeded and sliced
- 1 tbsp plain flour
- 600 ml/1 pint chicken stock
- 1 tbsp medium–hot Indian curry paste
- 115 g/4 oz ready-to-eat dried apricots
- salt and pepper
- baby spinach leaves and cooked couscous, to serve

1 Heat the oil in a large frying pan. Add the chops and cook over a medium heat for 2–4 minutes on each side, until evenly browned. Remove with tongs and put them into the slow cooker.

2 Add the shallot, garlic and peppers to the pan, reduce the heat and cook, stirring occasionally, for 5 minutes, until softened. Stir in the flour and cook, stirring constantly, for 1 minute. Gradually stir in the stock, a little at a time, then add the curry paste and apricots. Bring to the boil, stirring occasionally.

3 Season to taste with salt and pepper and transfer the mixture to the slow cooker. Cover and cook on low for 8–9 hours, until the meat is tender. Transfer to warmed serving plates and serve immediately with baby spinach and couscous.

mexican pork chops

serves 4

- 4 pork chops, trimmed of excess fat
- 2 tbsp corn oil
- 450 g/1 lb canned pineapple chunks in juice
- 1 red pepper, deseeded and finely chopped
- 2 fresh jalapeño chillies, deseeded and finely chopped
- 1 onion, finely chopped
- 1 tbsp chopped fresh coriander, plus extra sprigs to garnish
- 125 ml/4 fl oz hot chicken stock
- salt and pepper
- flour tortillas, to serve

1 Season the chops with salt and pepper to taste. Heat the oil in a large heavy-based frying pan. Add the chops and cook over a medium heat for 2–3 minutes each side, until lightly browned. Transfer them to the slow cooker. Drain the pineapple, reserving the juice, and set aside.

2 Add the red pepper, chillies and onion to the pan and cook, stirring occasionally, for 5 minutes, until the onion is softened. Transfer the mixture to the slow cooker and add the chopped coriander, stock and 125 ml/4 fl oz of the reserved pineapple juice. Cover and cook on low for 6 hours, until the chops are tender.

3 Add the reserved pineapple to the slow cooker, re-cover and cook on high for 15 minutes. Garnish with coriander sprigs and serve immediately with flour tortillas.

slow roast chicken

serves 4-6

- 1.5 kg/3 lb 5 oz oven-ready chicken
- ½ lemon
- 1 tbsp olive oil
- ½ tsp dried thyme
- ½ tsp paprika
- salt and pepper

1 Wipe the chicken with absorbent kitchen paper and tuck the lemon half inside the body cavity. Brush the oil over the chicken skin and sprinkle with thyme, paprika and salt and pepper, rubbing in with your fingers to cover all the skin.

2 Place the chicken in the slow cooker, cover and cook on high for 3 hours. Reduce the heat to low and cook for a further 4 hours, until the chicken is tender.

3 Carefully remove the chicken from the slow cooker and place on a warmed platter. Skim any fat from the juices and spoon over the chicken. Adjust the seasoning to taste and serve.

spicy chicken & bean stew

serves 4–6

- 200 g/7 oz dried haricot beans, soaked overnight, or for at least 5 hours
- 1 large onion, sliced
- 1 dried chipotle pepper, soaked for 20 minutes, then drained and finely chopped
- 1.5 kg/3 lb 5 oz oven-ready chicken
- 200 ml/7 fl oz hot chicken stock .
- 400 g/14 oz canned chopped tomatoes
- 1 tsp ground cumin
- salt and pepper

1 Drain and rinse the haricot beans, place in a saucepan, cover with fresh cold water and bring to the boil. Boil rapidly for at least 10 minutes, then remove from the heat, drain and rinse again.

2 Transfer the beans to the slow cooker and add the onion and chipotle pepper. Place the chicken on top, pour over the stock and tomatoes with their can juices, sprinkle with cumin and season to taste with salt and pepper.

3 Cover and cook on high for 4 hours. Carefully remove the chicken and cut into eight pieces. Skim the excess fat from the juices and adjust the seasoning.

4 Spoon the beans into a warmed serving dish, top with the chicken and spoon the juices over. Serve immediately.

chicken & apple pot

serves 4

- 1 tbsp olive oil
- 4 chicken portions, about 175 g/6 oz each
- 1 onion, chopped
- 2 celery sticks, roughly chopped
- 1½ tbsp plain flour
- 300 ml/10 fl oz clear apple juice
- 150 ml/5 fl oz chicken stock
- 1 cooking apple, cored and cut into quarters
- 2 bay leaves
- 1–2 tsp clear honey
- 1 yellow pepper, deseeded and cut into chunks
- salt and pepper

to garnish

- 1 large or 2 medium eating apples, cored and sliced
- 1 tbsp melted butter
- 2 tbsp demerara sugar
- 1 tbsp chopped fresh mint

1 Heat the oil in a heavy-based frying pan. Add the chicken and cook over a medium–high heat, turning frequently, for 10 minutes, until golden brown. Transfer to the slow cooker. Add the onion and celery to the pan and cook over a low heat for 5 minutes, until softened. Sprinkle in the flour and cook for 2 minutes, then remove the pan from the heat.

2 Gradually stir in the apple juice and stock, then return the pan to the heat and bring to the boil. Stir in the cooking apple, bay leaves and honey and season to taste. Pour the mixture over the chicken in the slow cooker, cover and cook on low for 6½ hours, until the chicken is tender and cooked through. Stir in the pepper, re-cover and cook on high for 45 minutes.

3 Shortly before serving, preheat the grill. Brush one side of the eating apple slices with half the melted butter and sprinkle with half the sugar. Cook under the preheated grill for 2–3 minutes, until the sugar has caramelized. Turn the slices over with tongs, brush with the remaining butter and sprinkle with the remaining sugar. Grill for a further 2 minutes. Transfer the stew to warmed plates and garnish with the caramelized apple slices and the mint. Serve immediately.

chicken & dumplings

serves 4
- 2 tbsp olive oil
- 1 large onion, thinly sliced
- 2 carrots, cut into 2-cm/ ¾-inch chunks
- 225 g/8 oz French beans, cut into 2.5-cm/1-inch lengths
- 4 skinless, boneless chicken breasts
- 300 ml/10 fl oz hot chicken stock
- salt and pepper

dumplings
- 200 g/7 oz self-raising flour
- 100 g/3½ oz shredded suet
- 4 tbsp chopped parsley

1 Heat 1 tablespoon of the oil in a frying pan, add the onion and fry over a high heat for 3–4 minutes, or until golden. Place in the slow cooker with the carrots and beans.

2 Add the remaining oil to the pan, then add the chicken breasts and fry until golden, turning once. Arrange on top of the vegetables in a single layer, season well with salt and pepper and pour over the stock. Cover and cook on low for 4 hours.

3 Turn the slow cooker up to high while making the dumplings. Sift the flour into a bowl and stir in the suet and parsley. Season to taste with salt and pepper. Stir in just enough cold water to make a fairly firm dough, mixing lightly. Divide into 12 and shape into small balls.

4 Arrange the dumplings on top of the chicken, cover and cook for 30 minutes on high. Transfer to warmed serving plates and serve immediately.

easy chinese chicken

serves 4

- 2 tsp grated fresh ginger
- 4 garlic cloves, finely chopped
- 2 star anise
- 150 ml/5 fl oz Chinese rice wine or medium-dry sherry
- 2 tbsp dark soy sauce
- 1 tsp sesame oil
- 5 tbsp water
- 4 skinless chicken thighs or drumsticks
- shredded spring onions, to garnish
- cooked rice, to serve

1 Mix the ginger, garlic, star anise, rice wine, soy sauce, sesame oil and water together in a bowl. Place the chicken in a saucepan, add the spice mixture and bring to the boil.

2 Transfer to the slow cooker, cover and cook on low for 4 hours, or until the chicken is tender and cooked through.

3 Remove and discard the star anise. Transfer the chicken to warmed serving plates, garnish with shredded spring onions and serve immediately with rice.

parmesan chicken

serves 4
- 1 egg, beaten
- 4 skinless, boneless chicken breasts
- 85 g/3 oz fine dry breadcrumbs
- 2 tbsp olive oil
- 350 g/12 oz ready-prepared tomato-based pasta sauce
- 4 thin slices Cheddar cheese
- 115 g/4 oz finely grated Parmesan cheese
- salt and pepper
- cooked rice, to serve

1 Season the egg with salt and pepper. Dip each chicken breast in the egg, turning to coat evenly, then dip into the breadcrumbs, pressing down lightly to cover evenly.

2 Heat the oil in a frying pan over a high heat. Add the chicken breasts and fry quickly for 3–4 minutes, until golden brown, turning once.

3 Pour the pasta sauce into the slow cooker and place the chicken breasts on top. Cover and cook on low for 4 hours.

4 Place a slice of Cheddar cheese on top of each chicken breast and sprinkle with Parmesan cheese. Cover and cook on high for a further 20 minutes. Transfer to a warmed serving dish and serve immediately with rice.

turkey meatloaf

serves 4

- oil, for greasing
- 600 g/1 lb 5 oz turkey mince
- 1 onion, finely chopped
- 55 g/2 oz porridge oats
- 2 tbsp chopped fresh sage
- 2 tbsp Worcestershire sauce
- 1 egg, beaten
- salt and pepper

1 Grease and line a 900-g/2-lb loaf tin, or a tin that fits into your slow cooker.

2 Mix the remaining ingredients together and season with salt and pepper.

3 Spoon the mixture into the tin and smooth the top level with a palette knife.

4 Place the loaf in the slow cooker and place a piece of greaseproof paper on top. Cover and cook on low for 4 hours, until firm and the juices are clear, not pink.

5 Turn out the loaf and serve sliced.

turkey & rice casserole

serves 4

- 1 tbsp olive oil
- 500 g/1 lb 2 oz diced turkey breast
- 1 onion, diced
- 2 carrots, diced
- 2 celery sticks, sliced
- 250 g/9 oz closed-cup mushrooms, sliced
- 175 g/6 oz long-grain rice, preferably Basmati
- 450 ml/16 fl oz hot chicken stock
- salt and pepper

1 Heat the oil in a heavy-based frying pan, add the turkey and fry over a high heat for 3–4 minutes, until lightly browned.

2 Combine the onion, carrots, celery, mushrooms and rice in the slow cooker. Arrange the turkey on top, season well with salt and pepper and pour the stock over. Cover and cook on high for 2 hours.

3 Stir lightly with a fork to mix, adjust the seasoning to taste and serve immediately.

turkey hash

serves 4

- 1 tbsp olive oil
- 500 g/1 lb 2 oz turkey mince
- 1 large red onion, diced
- 550 g/1 lb 4 oz butternut squash, diced
- 2 celery sticks, sliced
- 500 g/1 lb 2 oz potatoes, peeled and diced
- 3 tbsp Worcestershire sauce
- 2 bay leaves
- salt and pepper

1 Heat the oil in a frying pan, add the turkey and fry over a high heat, stirring, until broken up and lightly browned.

2 Place all the vegetables in the slow cooker then add the turkey and pan juices. Add the Worcestershire sauce and bay leaves and season with salt and pepper. Cover and cook on low for 7 hours. Remove the bay leaves, transfer to warmed serving bowls and serve immediately.

tagliatelle with prawns

serves 4
- 400 g/14 oz tomatoes, peeled and chopped
- 140 g/5 oz tomato purée
- 1 garlic clove, finely chopped
- 2 tbsp chopped fresh parsley
- 500 g/1 lb 2 oz cooked, peeled Mediterranean prawns
- 6 fresh basil leaves, torn, plus extra to garnish
- 400 g/14 oz dried tagliatelle
- salt and pepper

1 Put the tomatoes, tomato purée, garlic and parsley in the slow cooker and season with salt and pepper. Cover and cook on low for 7 hours.

2 Add the prawns and basil. Re-cover and cook on high for 15 minutes.

3 Meanwhile, bring a large saucepan of lightly salted water to the boil. Add the pasta, bring back to the boil and cook for 10–12 minutes, or until tender but still firm to the bite.

4 Drain the pasta and tip it into a warmed serving bowl. Add the prawn sauce and toss lightly with 2 large forks. Garnish with basil leaves and serve immediately.

shellfish stew

serves 8
- 1 tbsp olive oil
- 115 g/4 oz bacon, diced
- 2 tbsp butter
- 2 shallots, chopped
- 2 leeks, sliced
- 2 celery sticks, chopped
- 2 potatoes, diced
- 675 g/1 lb 8 oz tomatoes, peeled, deseeded and chopped
- 3 tbsp chopped fresh parsley
- 3 tbsp snipped fresh chives, plus extra to garnish
- 1 bay leaf
- 1 fresh thyme sprig
- 1.4 litres/2½ pints fish stock
- 24 live mussels
- 24 live clams
- 450 g/1 lb sea bream fillets
- 24 raw tiger prawns
- salt and pepper

1 Heat the oil in a heavy-based frying pan. Add the bacon and cook on a high heat, stirring frequently, for 5–8 minutes, until crisp. Using a slotted spoon, transfer to the slow cooker. Add the butter to the pan and when it has melted, add the shallots, leeks, celery and potatoes. Cook over a low heat, stirring occasionally, for 5 minutes, until softened. Stir in the tomatoes, parsley, chives, bay leaf and thyme, pour in the stock and bring to the boil, stirring constantly. Pour the mixture into the slow cooker, cover and cook on low for 7 hours.

2 Meanwhile, scrub the mussels and clams under cold running water and pull off the 'beards' from the mussels. Discard any with broken shells or that do not shut immediately when sharply tapped. Cut the fish fillets into bite-sized chunks. Peel and devein the prawns.

3 Remove the bay leaf and thyme sprig from the stew and discard. Season with salt and pepper and add all the fish and seafood. Re-cover and cook on high for 30 minutes. Discard any shellfish that remain closed. Garnish with chives and serve immediately.

salmon with dill & lime

serves 4

- 40 g/1½ oz butter, melted
- 1 onion, thinly sliced
- 450 g/1 lb potatoes, peeled and thinly sliced
- 100 ml/3½ fl oz hot fish stock or water
- 4 pieces skinless salmon fillet, about 140 g/5 oz each
- juice of 1 lime
- 2 tbsp chopped fresh dill
- salt and pepper
- lime wedges, to serve

1 Brush the base of the slow cooker with 1 tablespoon of the butter. Layer the onion and potatoes in the dish, sprinkling with salt and pepper between the layers. Add the stock and drizzle with 1 tablespoon of the butter. Cover and cook on low for 3 hours.

2 Arrange the salmon over the vegetables in a single layer. Drizzle the lime juice over, sprinkle with dill and salt and pepper, and pour the remaining butter on top. Cover and cook on low for a further 1 hour, until the fish flakes easily.

3 Serve the salmon and vegetables on warmed plates with the juices spooned over and lime wedges on the side.

salmon florentine

serves 4

- 150 ml/5 fl oz fish stock
- 225 ml/8 fl oz dry white wine
- 2 lemons
- 1 onion, thinly sliced
- 4 salmon fillets, about 175 g/6 oz each
- 1 bouquet garni
- 1.3 kg/3 lb spinach, coarse stalks removed
- freshly grated nutmeg, to taste
- 175 g/6 oz unsalted butter, plus extra for greasing
- salt and pepper

1 Lightly grease the slow cooker pot with butter. Pour the stock and wine into a saucepan and bring to the boil. Meanwhile, thinly slice one of the lemons. Put half the lemon slices and all the onion slices over the base of the slow cooker pot and top with the salmon fillets. Season to taste with salt and pepper, add the bouquet garni and cover the fish with the remaining lemon slices. Pour the hot stock mixture over the fish, cover and cook on low for 1½ hours, until the fish flakes easily.

2 Meanwhile, finely grate the rind and squeeze the juice from the remaining lemon. When the fish is nearly ready, cook the spinach in the water clinging to the leaves after washing, for 3–5 minutes, until wilted. Drain well, squeezing out as much water as possible. Arrange on a warmed serving dish and season to taste with nutmeg and salt and pepper.

3 Carefully lift the fish out of the slow cooker with a fish slice and discard the lemon slices, onion slices and bouquet garni. Put the salmon fillets on the bed of spinach and keep warm.

4 Melt the butter in a saucepan over a low heat. Stir in the lemon rind and half the juice. Taste and adjust the seasoning, adding more lemon juice and salt and pepper if needed. Pour the lemon butter sauce over the fish and serve immediately.

sea bream in lemon sauce

serves 4
- 8 sea bream fillets
- 55 g/2 oz unsalted butter
- 25 g/1 oz plain flour
- 850 ml/1½ pints warm milk
- 4 tbsp lemon juice
- 225 g/8 oz mushrooms, sliced
- 1 bouquet garni
- salt and pepper
- lemon wedges and griddled asparagus, to serve

1 Put the fish fillets into the slow cooker and set aside.

2 Melt the butter in a saucepan over a low heat. Add the flour and cook, stirring constantly, for 1 minute. Gradually stir in the milk, a little at a time, and bring to the boil, stirring constantly. Stir in the lemon juice and mushrooms, add the bouquet garni and season to taste with salt and pepper. Reduce the heat and simmer for 5 minutes. Pour the sauce over the fish fillets, cover and cook on low for 1½ hours.

3 Remove the bouquet garni. Carefully lift out the fish fillets and transfer to warmed serving plates. Serve immediately with lemon wedges and asparagus.

pollock bake

serves 4

- 1 tbsp olive oil
- 1 red onion, sliced
- 1 yellow pepper, deseeded and sliced
- 4 pollock fillets, about 140 g/5 oz each
- 2 tomatoes, thinly sliced
- 8 stoned black olives, halved
- 1 garlic clove, thinly sliced
- 2 tsp balsamic vinegar
- juice of 1 orange
- salt and pepper

1 Heat the oil in a frying pan, add the onion and yellow pepper and fry over a high heat for 3–4 minutes, stirring, until lightly browned. Transfer to the slow cooker, cover and cook on high for 1 hour.

2 Arrange the fish fillets over the vegetables and season with salt and pepper. Arrange a layer of tomatoes and olives over the top and sprinkle with the garlic, vinegar and salt and pepper. Pour over the orange juice, cover and cook on high for a further 1 hour. Transfer to warmed serving plates and serve immediately.

baked aubergine with courgette

serves 4

- 2 large aubergines
- olive oil, for brushing
- 2 large courgettes, sliced
- 4 tomatoes, sliced
- 1 garlic clove, finely chopped
- 15 g/½ oz dry breadcrumbs
- 15 g/½ oz Parmesan cheese, grated
- salt and pepper
- basil leaves, to garnish

1 Cut the aubergines into fairly thin slices and brush with oil. Heat a large griddle pan or heavy-based frying pan over a high heat, then add the aubergines and cook in batches for 6–8 minutes, turning once, until softened and browned.

2 Layer the aubergines in the slow cooker with the courgettes, tomatoes and garlic, seasoning with salt and pepper between the layers.

3 Mix the breadcrumbs with the cheese and sprinkle over the vegetables. Cover and cook on low for 4 hours.

4 Transfer to warmed serving bowls, garnish with basil leaves and serve immediately.

summer vegetable casserole

serves 4

- 400 g/14 oz canned cannellini beans, drained and rinsed
- 400 g/14 oz canned artichoke hearts, drained
- 1 red pepper, deseeded and sliced
- 4 small turnips, sliced
- 225 g/8 oz baby spinach leaves, coarse stalks removed
- 6 fresh thyme sprigs
- 400 g/14 oz frozen baby broad beans
- 1 tbsp olive oil
- 25 g/1 oz butter
- 4 shallots, chopped
- 4 leeks, sliced
- 3 celery sticks, sliced
- 3 tbsp plain flour
- 200 ml/7 fl oz dry white wine
- 150 ml/5 fl oz vegetable stock
- salt and pepper

1 Put the cannellini beans, artichoke hearts, red pepper, turnips, spinach and four of the thyme sprigs into the slow cooker.

2 Cook the broad beans in a small saucepan of lightly salted boiling water for 10 minutes.

3 Meanwhile, heat the oil and butter in a large frying pan. Add the shallots, leeks and celery and cook over a low heat, stirring occasionally, for 5 minutes, until softened. Stir in the flour and cook, stirring constantly, for 1 minute. Gradually stir in the wine and stock and bring to the boil, stirring constantly. Season to taste with salt and pepper.

4 Transfer the contents of the frying pan to the slow cooker. Drain the broad beans and add to the slow cooker. Stir well, cover and cook on low for 2½–3 hours. Remove and discard the thyme sprigs. Transfer to warmed serving dishes and garnish with the remaining thyme sprigs. Serve immediately.

spring stew

serves 4

- 225 g/8 oz dried haricot beans, soaked overnight, or for at least 5 hours
- 2 tbsp olive oil
- 4–8 baby onions, halved
- 2 celery sticks, cut into 5-mm/¼-inch slices
- 225 g/8 oz young carrots, halved if large
- 300 g/10½ oz new potatoes, halved
- 850 ml–1.2 litres/1½–2 pints vegetable stock
- 1 bouquet garni
- 1½–2 tbsp light soy sauce
- 85 g/3 oz baby sweetcorn
- 115 g/4 oz shelled broad beans, thawed if frozen
- 225 g/8 oz Savoy cabbage, shredded
- 1½ tbsp cornflour
- salt and pepper
- 55–85 g/2–3 oz Parmesan cheese, grated, to serve

1 Drain and rinse the haricot beans, place in a saucepan, cover with fresh cold water and bring to the boil. Boil rapidly for at least 10 minutes, then remove from the heat, drain and rinse again.

2 Heat the oil in a saucepan. Add the onions, celery, carrots and potatoes and cook over a low heat, stirring frequently, for 5–8 minutes until softened. Add the stock, haricot beans, bouquet garni and soy sauce, bring to the boil, then transfer to the slow cooker.

3 Add the sweetcorn, broad beans and cabbage, season with salt and pepper and stir well. Cover and cook on high for 3–4 hours, until the vegetables are tender.

4 Remove and discard the bouquet garni. Stir the cornflour and 3 tablespoons of water to a paste in a small bowl, then stir into the stew. Re-cover and cook on high for a further 15 minutes until thickened. Serve the stew with the cheese.

mixed vegetable casserole

serves 4
- 500 g/1 lb 2 oz potatoes, peeled and cubed
- 2 courgettes, cubed
- 2 red peppers, deseeded and cubed
- 2 red onions, sliced
- 2 tsp mixed dried herbs
- 250 ml/9 fl oz hot vegetable stock
- salt and pepper

1 Layer all the vegetables in the slow cooker, sprinkling with herbs and salt and pepper between the layers.

2 Pour over the stock. Cover and cook on low for 7 hours. Transfer to warmed serving bowls and serve immediately.

parsley dumpling stew

serves 6

- ½ swede, cut into chunks
- 2 onions, sliced
- 2 potatoes, cut into chunks
- 2 carrots, cut into chunks
- 2 celery sticks, sliced
- 2 courgettes, sliced
- 2 tbsp tomato purée
- 600 ml/1 pint hot vegetable stock
- 1 bay leaf
- 1 tsp ground coriander
- ½ tsp dried thyme
- 400 g/14 oz canned sweetcorn, drained
- salt and pepper

parsley dumplings

- 200 g/7 oz self-raising flour
- pinch of salt
- 115 g/4 oz vegetable suet
- 2 tbsp chopped fresh flat-leaf parsley, plus extra sprigs to garnish
- about 125 ml/4 fl oz milk

1 Put the swede, onions, potatoes, carrots, celery and courgettes into the slow cooker. Stir the tomato purée into the stock and pour it over the vegetables. Add the bay leaf, coriander and thyme and season to taste with salt and pepper. Cover and cook on low for 6 hours.

2 To make the dumplings, sift the flour with the salt into a bowl and stir in the suet and chopped parsley. Add just enough of the milk to make a firm but light dough. Knead lightly and shape into 12 small balls.

3 Stir the sweetcorn into the mixture in the slow cooker and place the dumplings on top. Cook on high for 30 minutes. Remove the bay leaf. Transfer to warmed serving plates, garnish with parsley sprigs and serve immediately.

vegetable pasta

serves 4

- 250 g/9 oz dried penne pasta
- 2 tbsp olive oil, plus extra for drizzling
- 1 red onion, sliced
- 2 courgettes, thinly sliced
- 200 g/7 oz closed cup mushrooms, sliced
- 2 tbsp chopped fresh oregano
- 300 g/10½ oz tomatoes, sliced
- 55 g/2 oz Parmesan cheese, grated
- salt and pepper

1 Bring a large saucepan of lightly salted water to the boil. Add the pasta, bring back to the boil and cook for 8–10 minutes, or until tender but still firm to the bite. Drain.

2 Meanwhile, heat the oil in a heavy-based saucepan, add the onions and cook over a medium heat, stirring occasionally, for 5 minutes, until softened. Stir into the pasta.

3 Place a layer of courgettes and mushrooms in the slow cooker and top with a layer of pasta. Sprinkle with oregano and salt and pepper, and continue layering, finishing with a layer of vegetables.

4 Arrange the sliced tomatoes on top and drizzle with oil. Cover and cook on high for 3 hours, or until tender.

5 Sprinkle with the cheese, cover and cook for a further 10 minutes. Transfer to a warmed serving bowl and serve immediately.

vegetable curry

serves 4–6

- 2 tbsp vegetable oil
- 1 tsp cumin seeds
- 1 onion, sliced
- 2 curry leaves
- 2.5-cm/1-inch piece fresh ginger, finely chopped
- 2 fresh red chillies, deseeded and chopped
- 2 tbsp Indian curry paste
- 2 carrots, sliced
- 115 g/4 oz mangetout
- 1 cauliflower, cut into florets
- 3 tomatoes, peeled and chopped
- 85 g/3 oz frozen peas, thawed
- ½ tsp ground turmeric
- 150–225 ml/5–8 fl oz hot vegetable stock
- salt and pepper
- naan breads, to serve

1 Heat the oil in a large heavy-based saucepan. Add the cumin seeds and cook on a medium–high heat, stirring constantly, for 1–2 minutes, until they give off their aroma and begin to pop. Add the onion and curry leaves and cook, stirring occasionally, for 5 minutes, until the onion has softened. Add the ginger and chillies and cook, stirring occasionally, for 1 minute.

2 Stir in the curry paste and cook, stirring, for 2 minutes, then add the carrots, mangetout and cauliflower. Cook for 5 minutes, then add the tomatoes, peas and turmeric, and season to taste with salt and pepper. Cook for 3 minutes, then add 150 ml/5 fl oz of the stock and bring to the boil.

3 Transfer the mixture to the slow cooker. If the vegetables are not covered by the liquid, add more hot stock, then cover and cook on low for 5 hours, until tender. Remove and discard the curry leaves. Transfer to warmed serving dishes and serve immediately with naan breads.

asparagus & spinach risotto

serves 4

- 2 tbsp olive oil
- 4 shallots, finely chopped
- 280 g/10 oz arborio rice
- 1 garlic clove, crushed
- 100 ml/3½ fl oz dry white wine
- 850 ml/1½ pints vegetable stock
- 200 g/7 oz asparagus spears
- 200 g/7 oz baby spinach leaves
- 40 g/1½ oz Parmesan cheese, grated
- salt and pepper

1 Heat the oil in a frying pan, add the shallots and fry over a medium heat, stirring, for 2–3 minutes. Add the rice and garlic and cook for a further 2 minutes, stirring. Add the wine and allow it to boil for 30 seconds.

2 Transfer the rice mixture to the slow cooker, add the stock and season to taste with salt and pepper. Cover and cook on high for 2 hours, or until most of the liquid is absorbed.

3 Cut the asparagus into 4.5-cm/1¾-inch lengths. Stir into the rice, then spread the spinach over the top. Replace the lid and cook on high for a further 30 minutes, until the asparagus is just tender and the spinach is wilted.

4 Stir in the spinach with the cheese, then adjust the seasoning to taste. Serve immediately in warmed bowls.

Enjoy
entertaining

beef bourguignon

serves 6

- 2 tbsp plain flour
- 900 g/2 lb braising steak, trimmed and cut into 2.5-cm/1-inch cubes
- 6 rashers streaky bacon, derinded and chopped
- 3 tbsp olive oil
- 25 g/1 oz unsalted butter
- 12 baby onions or shallots
- 2 garlic cloves, finely chopped
- 150 ml/5 fl oz beef stock
- 450 ml/16 fl oz full-bodied red wine
- 1 bouquet garni
- 140 g/5 oz mushrooms, quartered
- salt and pepper

1 Put the flour into a plastic food bag and season to taste with salt and pepper. Add the steak cubes, in batches, hold the top securely and shake well to coat. Transfer the meat to a plate.

2 Place the bacon in a large heavy-based saucepan and cook on a high heat, stirring occasionally, until crisp. Using a slotted spoon, transfer the bacon to a plate. Add the oil to the pan. When it is hot, add the steak cubes and cook, in batches, stirring occasionally, for 5 minutes, until evenly browned. Transfer to the plate with a slotted spoon.

3 Add the butter to the pan. When it has melted, add the onions and garlic and cook, stirring occasionally, for 5 minutes. Return the bacon and steak to the pan and pour in the stock and wine. Bring to the boil.

4 Transfer the mixture to the slow cooker and add the bouquet garni. Cover and cook on low for 7 hours, until the meat is tender.

5 Add the mushrooms to the slow cooker and stir well. Re-cover and cook on high for 15 minutes.

6 Remove and discard the bouquet garni. Taste and adjust the seasoning, adding salt and pepper if needed. Transfer to warmed serving bowls and serve immediately.

pot roast with beer

serves 4–6

- 2 small onions, each cut into 8 wedges
- 8 small carrots, halved lengthways
- 1 fennel bulb, cut into 8 wedges
- 2.25 kg/5 lb rolled chuck steak
- 2 tbsp Dijon mustard
- 1 tbsp plain flour
- 100 ml/3½ fl oz beer
- salt and pepper

1 Place the onions, carrots and fennel in the slow cooker and season to taste with salt and pepper. Place the beef on top.

2 Mix the mustard and flour together to form a paste and spread it over the beef. Season well and pour over the beer. Cover and cook on low for 8 hours.

3 Remove the beef and vegetables with a slotted spoon and transfer to a warmed serving platter. Skim the excess fat from the juices and pour the juices into a jug to serve with the beef. Serve immediately.

hungarian goulash

serves 4

- 4 tbsp sunflower oil
- 650 g/1 lb 7 oz braising steak, cut into 2.5-cm/ 1-inch cubes
- 2 tsp plain flour
- 2 tsp paprika
- 300 ml/10 fl oz beef stock
- 3 onions, chopped
- 4 carrots, diced
- 1 large potato or 2 medium potatoes, diced
- 1 bay leaf
- ½–1 tsp caraway seeds
- 400 g/14 oz canned chopped tomatoes
- 2 tbsp soured cream
- salt and pepper

1 Heat half the oil in a heavy-based frying pan. Add the beef and cook over a medium heat, stirring frequently, until evenly browned. Reduce the heat and stir in the flour and paprika. Cook, stirring constantly, for 2 minutes. Gradually stir in the stock and bring to the boil, then transfer the mixture to the slow cooker.

2 Wipe out the pan with kitchen paper, then heat the remaining oil. Add the onions and cook over a low heat, stirring occasionally, for 5 minutes, until softened. Stir in the carrots and potato and cook for a further few minutes. Add the bay leaf, caraway seeds and tomatoes. Season to taste with salt and pepper.

3 Transfer the vegetable mixture to the slow cooker and stir well, then cover and cook on low for 9 hours, until the meat is tender.

4 Remove and discard the bay leaf. Stir in the soured cream and transfer to warmed serving plates. Serve immediately.

neapolitan beef

serves 6

- 300 ml/10 fl oz red wine
- 4 tbsp olive oil
- 1 celery stick, chopped
- 2 shallots, sliced
- 4 garlic cloves, finely chopped
- 1 bay leaf
- 10 fresh basil leaves, plus extra to garnish
- 3 fresh parsley sprigs
- pinch of grated nutmeg
- pinch of ground cinnamon
- 2 cloves
- 1.5 kg/3 lb 5 oz beef silverside, in one piece
- 1-2 garlic cloves, thinly sliced
- 55 g/2 oz streaky bacon or pancetta, derinded and chopped
- 400 g/14 oz canned chopped tomatoes
- 2 tbsp tomato purée

1 Combine the wine, half the oil, the celery, shallots, garlic, herbs and spices in a large non-metallic bowl. Add the beef, cover and leave to marinate, turning occasionally, for 12 hours.

2 Drain the beef, reserving the marinade, and pat dry with kitchen paper. Make small incisions all over the beef using a sharp knife. Insert a slice of garlic and a piece of bacon in each 'pocket'. Heat the remaining oil in a large frying pan. Add the meat and cook over a medium heat, turning frequently, until evenly browned. Transfer to the slow cooker.

3 Strain the reserved marinade into the pan and bring to the boil. Stir in the tomatoes and tomato purée. Stir well, then pour the mixture over the beef. Cover and cook on low for about 8–9 hours, until the beef is cooked to your liking. If possible, turn the beef over halfway through the cooking time.

4 Remove and discard the bay leaf. Remove the beef from the slow cooker and place on a carving board. Cover with foil and leave to stand for 10–15 minutes to firm up. Cut into slices and transfer to a platter. Spoon over the sauce, garnish with basil leaves and serve immediately.

caribbean beef stew

serves 6

- 450 g/1 lb braising steak
- 450 g/1 lb diced pumpkin or other squash
- 1 onion, chopped
- 1 red pepper, deseeded and chopped
- 2 garlic cloves, finely chopped
- 2.5-cm/1-inch piece fresh ginger, finely chopped
- 1 tbsp sweet or hot paprika
- 225 ml/8 fl oz beef stock
- 400 g/14 oz canned chopped tomatoes
- 400 g/14 oz canned pigeon peas or chickpeas, drained and rinsed
- 400 g/14 oz canned black-eyed beans, drained and rinsed
- salt and pepper

1 Trim off any visible fat from the steak, then dice the meat. Heat a large heavy-based saucepan without adding any extra fat. Add the meat and cook, stirring constantly, for a few minutes, until evenly browned. Stir in the pumpkin, onion and red pepper and cook for 1 minute, then add the garlic, ginger and paprika. Pour in the stock and tomatoes and bring to the boil.

2 Transfer the mixture to the slow cooker, cover and cook on low for 7 hours. Add the pigeon peas and black-eyed beans to the stew and season to taste with salt and pepper. Re-cover and cook on high for 30 minutes. Transfer to warmed serving bowls and serve immediately.

beef in coffee sauce

serves 6

- 4 tbsp sunflower oil
- 1.3 kg/3 lb braising steak, cut into 2.5-cm/1-inch cubes
- 4 onions, sliced
- 1 garlic clove, finely chopped
- 5 tbsp plain flour
- 300 ml/10 fl oz red wine
- pinch of dried oregano
- 1 small fresh rosemary sprig
- 500 ml/18 fl oz black coffee
- salt and pepper
- fresh marjoram sprigs, to garnish
- mashed sweet potatoes, to serve

1 Heat the oil in a large frying pan. Add the steak cubes and cook over a medium heat, stirring frequently, for 8–10 minutes, until evenly browned. Transfer to the slow cooker with a slotted spoon.

2 Add the onions and garlic to the pan, reduce the heat and cook, stirring occasionally, for 10 minutes, until softened and just beginning to colour. Stir in the flour and cook, stirring constantly, for 1 minute. Gradually stir in the wine, a little at a time. Add the oregano and rosemary and season to taste with salt and pepper. Pour in the coffee and bring to the boil, stirring constantly.

3 Transfer the mixture to the slow cooker. Cover and cook on low for 8–9 hours, until the meat is tender. Remove and discard the rosemary sprig. Taste and adjust the seasoning, adding salt and pepper if needed. Transfer to warmed serving plates, garnish with marjoram sprigs and serve immediately with mashed sweet potatoes.

venison casserole

serves 6

- 3 tbsp olive oil
- 1 kg/2 lb 4 oz braising venison, cut into 3-cm/ 1¼-cm cubes
- 2 onions, thinly sliced
- 2 garlic cloves, chopped
- 350 ml/12 fl oz beef stock
- 2 tbsp plain flour
- 125 ml/4 fl oz port
- 2 tbsp redcurrant jelly
- 6 juniper berries, crushed
- 4 cloves, crushed
- pinch of ground cinnamon
- pinch of freshly grated nutmeg
- salt and pepper
- chopped fresh flat-leaf parsley, to garnish
- mashed potatoes, to serve

1 Heat the oil in a heavy-based pan. Add the venison and cook over a high heat, stirring frequently, for 5 minutes, until browned all over. Using a slotted spoon, transfer the meat to the slow cooker.

2 Add the onions and garlic to the pan, reduce the heat and cook, stirring occasionally, for 5 minutes, until softened. Transfer them to the slow cooker.

3 Gradually stir the stock into the pan, scraping up any sediment from the base, then bring to the boil, stirring constantly. Sprinkle the flour over the meat in the slow cooker and stir well to coat evenly. Stir in the hot stock, then stir in the port, redcurrant jelly, juniper berries, cloves, cinnamon and nutmeg. Season to taste with salt and pepper. Cover and cook on low for 7–8 hours, until the meat is tender.

4 Taste and adjust the seasoning, adding salt and pepper if needed. Remove and discard the cloves. Garnish with parsley and serve immediately with mashed potatoes.

lamb tagine

serves 6

- 3 tbsp olive oil
- 2 red onions, chopped
- 2 garlic cloves, finely chopped
- 2.5-cm/1-inch piece fresh ginger, finely chopped
- 1 yellow pepper, deseeded and chopped
- 1 kg/2 lb 4 oz boneless shoulder of lamb, trimmed and cut into 2.5-cm/1-inch cubes
- 850 ml/1½ pints lamb or chicken stock
- 225 g/8 oz ready-to-eat dried apricots, halved
- 1 tbsp clear honey
- 4 tbsp lemon juice
- pinch of saffron threads
- 5-cm/2-inch cinnamon stick
- salt and pepper
- toasted flaked almonds and fresh coriander sprigs, to garnish

1 Heat the oil in a large heavy-based saucepan. Add the onions, garlic, ginger and yellow pepper and cook over a low heat, stirring occasionally, for 5 minutes, until the onion has softened. Add the lamb and stir well to mix, then pour in the stock. Add the apricots, honey, lemon juice, saffron and cinnamon stick and season to taste with salt and pepper. Bring to the boil.

2 Transfer the mixture to the slow cooker. Cover and cook on low for 8½ hours, until the meat is tender.

3 Remove and discard the cinnamon stick. Transfer to warmed serving bowls and garnish with flaked almonds and coriander sprigs. Serve immediately.

sausage & bean cassoulet

serves 4

- 2 tbsp sunflower oil
- 2 onions, chopped
- 2 garlic cloves, finely chopped
- 115 g/4 oz rindless, streaky bacon, chopped
- 500 g/1 lb 2 oz pork sausages
- 400 g/14 oz canned haricot, red kidney or black-eyed beans, drained and rinsed
- 2 tbsp chopped fresh parsley
- 150 ml/5 fl oz hot beef stock
- 4 slices French bread
- 55 g/2 oz Gruyère cheese, grated

1 Heat the oil in a heavy-based frying pan. Add the onions and cook over a low heat, stirring occasionally, for 5 minutes, until softened. Add the garlic, bacon and sausages and cook, stirring and turning the sausages occasionally, for a further 5 minutes.

2 Using a slotted spoon, transfer the mixture from the frying pan to the slow cooker. Add the beans, parsley and stock, then cover and cook on low for 6 hours.

3 Shortly before serving, preheat the grill. Place the bread slices on the grill rack and lightly toast on one side under the preheated grill. Turn the slices over, sprinkle with the grated cheese and place under the grill until just melted.

4 Serve the cassoulet and the bread slices immediately.

pork with almonds

serves 4

- 2 tbsp corn or sunflower oil
- 2 onions, chopped
- 2 garlic cloves, finely chopped
- 5-cm/2-inch cinnamon stick
- 3 cloves
- 115 g/4 oz ground almonds
- 750 g/1 lb 10 oz boneless pork, cut into 2.5-cm/1-inch cubes
- 4 tomatoes, peeled and chopped
- 2 tbsp capers
- 115 g/4 oz green olives, stoned
- 3 pickled jalapeño chillies, drained, deseeded and cut into rings
- 350 ml/12 fl oz chicken stock
- salt and pepper

1 Heat half the oil in a large heavy-based frying pan. Add the onions and cook over a low heat, stirring occasionally, for 5 minutes, until softened. Add the garlic, cinnamon stick, cloves and almonds and cook, stirring frequently, for 8–10 minutes. Be careful not to burn the almonds.

2 Remove and discard the cinnamon stick and cloves and transfer the mixture to a food processor. Process to a smooth purée.

3 Wipe out the pan with kitchen paper, then return to the heat. Heat the remaining oil, then add the pork, in batches if necessary. Cook over a medium heat, stirring frequently, for 5–10 minutes, until evenly browned.

4 Add the almond purée, tomatoes, capers, olives, chillies and stock to the pan. Bring to the boil, then transfer to the slow cooker. Season to taste with salt and pepper and mix well. Cover and cook on low for 5 hours. Transfer to warmed plates and serve immediately.

chicken in riesling

serves 4-6

- 2 tbsp plain flour
- 1 chicken, weighing 1.6 kg/ 3 lb 8 oz, cut into 8 pieces
- 55 g/2 oz unsalted butter
- 1 tbsp sunflower oil
- 4 shallots, finely chopped
- 12 button mushrooms, sliced
- 2 tbsp brandy
- 500 ml/18 fl oz Riesling wine
- 250 ml/9 fl oz double cream
- salt and pepper
- cooked green vegetables, to serve

1 Put the flour into a plastic food bag and season to taste. Add the chicken pieces, in batches, hold the top securely and shake well to coat. Transfer the chicken to a plate.

2 Heat half the butter with the oil in a heavy-based frying pan. Add the chicken pieces and cook over a medium–high heat, turning frequently, for 10 minutes, until golden all over. Using a slotted spoon, transfer them to a plate.

3 Wipe out the pan with kitchen paper, then return to a medium–high heat and melt the remaining butter. Add the shallots and mushrooms and cook, stirring constantly, for 3 minutes. Return the chicken to the pan and remove it from the heat. Warm the brandy in a small ladle, ignite and pour it over the chicken, shaking the pan gently until the flames have died down.

4 Return the pan to the heat and pour in the wine. Bring to the boil over a low heat, scraping up any sediment from the base of the pan. Transfer to the slow cooker, cover and cook on low for 5–6 hours, until the chicken is tender and cooked through.

5 Transfer the chicken to a serving dish and keep warm. Skim off any fat from the surface of the cooking liquid and pour the liquid into a saucepan. Stir in the cream and bring just to the boil over a low heat. Pour over the chicken. Serve immediately with green vegetables.

chicken bonne femme

serves 6
- 1 chicken, weighing 1.8 kg/4 lb
- 55 g/2 oz butter
- 2 tbsp olive oil
- 650 g/1 lb 7 oz small white onions, peeled
- 650 g/1 lb 7 oz small new potatoes
- 175 g/6 oz bacon, diced
- 500 ml/18 fl oz dry white wine
- 1 bouquet garni
- 500 ml/18 fl oz hot chicken stock
- salt and pepper
- chopped fresh flat-leaf parsley, to garnish

1 Season the chicken inside and out with salt and pepper. Melt half the butter with the oil in a large frying pan. Add the chicken and cook over a medium heat, turning frequently, for 8–10 minutes, until evenly browned. Remove from the pan and put it into the slow cooker, breast-side down.

2 Add the onions, potatoes and bacon to the pan and cook, stirring frequently, for 10 minutes, until lightly browned. Pour in the wine, season to taste with salt and pepper and add the bouquet garni. Bring to the boil, then transfer the mixture to the slow cooker. Pour in the hot stock. Cover and cook, turning the chicken once halfway through cooking, for 5–6 hours, until the chicken is tender and cooked through.

3 Using a slotted spoon, transfer the vegetables and bacon to a warmed bowl. Carefully remove the chicken and put it on a warmed serving dish. Remove and discard the bouquet garni.

4 Measure 600 ml/1 pint of the cooking liquid, pour it into a saucepan and bring to the boil. Boil until slightly reduced, then whisk in the remaining butter, a little at a time. Pour the sauce into a sauceboat. Carve the chicken and transfer to individual plates with the bacon and vegetables. Garnish with parsley and serve immediately with the sauce.

bulgarian chicken

serves 6

- 2 tbsp sunflower oil
- 6 chicken portions
- 2 onions, chopped
- 2 garlic cloves, finely chopped
- 1 fresh red chilli, deseeded and finely chopped
- 6 tomatoes, peeled and chopped
- 2 tsp sweet paprika
- 1 bay leaf
- 225 ml/8 fl oz hot chicken stock
- salt and pepper

1 Heat the oil in a large heavy-based frying pan. Add the chicken and cook over a medium heat, turning occasionally, for about 10 minutes, until evenly browned.

2 Transfer the chicken to the slow cooker and add the onions, garlic, chilli and tomatoes. Sprinkle in the paprika, add the bay leaf and pour in the stock. Season to taste with salt and pepper. Stir well, cover and cook on low for 6 hours, until the chicken is cooked through and tender. Remove and discard the bay leaf. Transfer to warmed serving plates and serve immediately.

chicken parmigiana

serves 4

- 4 chicken portions, about 250 g/9 oz each
- 100 ml/3½ fl oz olive oil
- 3 red onions, thinly sliced
- 2 garlic cloves, finely chopped
- 1 red pepper, deseeded and thinly sliced
- 115 g/4 oz mushrooms, sliced
- 2 tsp chopped fresh thyme
- 1 tbsp chopped fresh flat-leaf parsley
- 400 g/14 oz canned chopped tomatoes
- 4 tbsp dry white vermouth
- 425 ml/15 fl oz chicken stock
- 85 g/3 oz Parmesan cheese, grated, to garnish
- salt and pepper
- cooked pappardelle, to serve

1 Season the chicken with salt and pepper to taste. Heat the oil in a large heavy-based saucepan. Add the chicken and cook over a medium heat for 5–6 minutes on each side, until evenly browned. Using tongs, transfer the chicken to the slow cooker.

2 Add the onions, garlic, red pepper, mushrooms, thyme, parsley, tomatoes, vermouth and stock to the pan. Season to taste with salt and pepper and bring to the boil, stirring occasionally. Transfer the mixture to the slow cooker, cover and cook on low for 8–9 hours, until the chicken is cooked through and tender.

3 Taste and adjust the seasoning, adding salt and pepper if needed. Transfer to warmed plates and sprinkle over the Parmesan cheese. Serve immediately with pappardelle.

nutty chicken

serves 4

- 3 tbsp sunflower oil
- 4 skinless chicken portions
- 2 shallots, chopped
- 1 tsp ground ginger
- 1 tbsp plain flour
- 425 ml/15 fl oz beef stock
- 55 g/2 oz walnut pieces
- grated rind of 1 lemon
- 2 tbsp lemon juice
- 1 tbsp black treacle
- salt and pepper
- pea shoots, to garnish

1 Heat the oil in a large heavy-based frying pan. Season the chicken portions with salt and pepper and add to the pan. Cook over a medium heat, turning occasionally, for 5–8 minutes, until lightly golden all over. Transfer to the slow cooker.

2 Add the shallots to the pan and cook, stirring occasionally, for 3–4 minutes, until softened. Sprinkle in the ginger and flour and cook, stirring constantly, for 1 minute. Gradually stir in the stock and bring to the boil, stirring constantly. Reduce the heat and simmer for 1 minute, then stir in the walnuts, lemon rind and juice and treacle.

3 Pour the sauce over the chicken. Cover and cook on low for 6 hours, until the chicken is cooked through and tender. Taste and adjust the seasoning, adding salt and pepper if needed. Transfer the chicken to warmed plates and spoon some of the sauce over each portion. Garnish with pea shoots and serve immediately.

chicken cacciatore

serves 4

- 3 tbsp olive oil
- 4 skinless chicken portions
- 2 onions, sliced
- 2 garlic cloves, finely chopped
- 400 g/14 oz canned chopped tomatoes
- 1 tbsp tomato purée
- 2 tbsp chopped fresh parsley
- 2 tsp fresh thyme leaves, plus extra sprigs to garnish
- 150 ml/5 fl oz red wine
- salt and pepper

1 Heat the oil in a heavy-based frying pan. Add the chicken and cook over a medium heat, turning occasionally, for 10 minutes, until golden all over. Using a slotted spoon, transfer the chicken to the slow cooker.

2 Add the onions to the pan and cook, stirring occasionally, for 5 minutes, until softened and just turning golden. Add the garlic, tomatoes, tomato purée, parsley, thyme leaves and wine. Season to taste with salt and pepper and bring to the boil.

3 Pour the tomato mixture over the chicken pieces. Cover and cook on low for 5 hours, until the chicken is tender and cooked through. Taste and adjust the seasoning, adding salt and pepper if needed. Transfer to warmed serving plates, garnish with thyme sprigs and serve immediately.

chicken braised with cabbage

serves 4

- 2 tbsp sunflower oil
- 4 skinless chicken thighs or drumsticks
- 1 onion, chopped
- 500 g/1 lb 2 oz red cabbage, cored and shredded
- 2 apples, peeled and chopped
- 12 canned or cooked chestnuts, halved (optional)
- ½ tsp juniper berries
- 125 ml/4 fl oz red wine
- salt and pepper
- chopped fresh flat-leaf parsley, to garnish

1 Heat the oil in a large heavy-based saucepan. Add the chicken and cook on a medium–high heat, turning frequently, for 5 minutes, until golden on all sides. Using a slotted spoon, transfer to a plate lined with kitchen paper.

2 Add the onion to the pan and cook over a medium heat, stirring occasionally, until softened. Stir in the cabbage and apples and cook, stirring occasionally, for 5 minutes. Add the chestnuts, if using, juniper berries and wine and season to taste with salt and pepper. Bring to the boil.

3 Spoon half the cabbage mixture into the slow cooker, add the chicken pieces, then top with the remaining cabbage mixture. Cover and cook on low for 5 hours, until the chicken is tender and cooked through. Transfer to warmed serving bowls, garnish with parsley and serve immediately.

pesto turkey pasta

serves 4

- 250 g/9 oz dried macaroni
- 175 ml/6 fl oz tomato juice
- 500 g/1 lb 2 oz turkey mince
- 1 small onion, finely chopped
- 40 g/1½ oz fresh white breadcrumbs
- 100 g/3½ oz pesto sauce
- 125 g/4½ oz mozzarella cheese
- salt and pepper
- fresh basil leaves, to garnish

1 Bring a large saucepan of lightly salted water to the boil, add the pasta, return to the boil and cook for half the amount of time stated on the packet (5–6 minutes). Drain well, place in the slow cooker and stir in the tomato juice.

2 Mix the turkey, onion and breadcrumbs together. Season well with salt and pepper. Divide the mixture into about 20 small balls, rolling them with your hands.

3 Arrange the meatballs over the pasta in a single layer and spoon a little of the pesto sauce on top of each. Cover and cook on high for 2 hours.

4 Tear the mozzarella cheese into small pieces and scatter over the meatballs. Cover and cook on high for a further 20 minutes. Serve immediately, garnished with fresh basil.

moroccan sea bass

serves 2

- 2 tbsp olive oil
- 2 onions, chopped
- 2 garlic cloves, finely chopped
- 2 carrots, finely chopped
- 1 fennel bulb, finely chopped
- ½ tsp ground cumin
- ½ tsp ground cloves
- 1 tsp ground coriander
- pinch of saffron threads
- 300 ml/10 fl oz fish stock
- 1 preserved or fresh lemon
- 900 g/2 lb sea bass, cleaned
- salt and pepper

1 Heat the oil in a large heavy-based saucepan. Add the onions, garlic, carrots and fennel and cook over a medium heat, stirring occasionally, for 5 minutes. Stir in all the spices and cook, stirring, for a further 2 minutes. Pour in the stock, season to taste with salt and pepper, and bring to the boil.

2 Transfer the mixture to the slow cooker. Cover and cook on low for 6 hours, or until the vegetables are tender.

3 Rinse the preserved lemon. Discard the fish head, if you like. Slice the lemon and place the slices in the fish cavity, then place the fish in the slow cooker on top of the vegetables. Re-cover and cook on high for 30–45 minutes, until the flesh flakes easily.

4 Carefully transfer the fish to a platter and spoon the vegetables around it, using a slotted spoon. Cover and keep warm. Transfer the cooking liquid to a saucepan and boil for a few minutes, until reduced. Spoon it over the fish and serve immediately.

red snapper with fennel

serves 4

- 4 whole red snapper, about 350 g/12 oz each, cleaned
- 1 orange, halved and thinly sliced
- 2 garlic cloves, thinly sliced
- 6 fresh thyme sprigs
- 1 tbsp olive oil
- 1 fennel bulb, thinly sliced
- 450 ml/16 fl oz orange juice
- 1 bay leaf
- 1 tsp dill seeds
- salt and pepper
- salad leaves, to serve

1 Season the fish inside and outside with salt and pepper. Make 3–4 diagonal slashes on each side. Divide the orange slices between the cavities and add 2–3 garlic slices and a thyme sprig to each. Put the remaining garlic and thyme in the slashes.

2 Heat the oil in a large frying pan. Add the fennel and cook over a medium heat, stirring frequently, for 3–5 minutes, until just softened. Add the orange juice and bay leaf, and bring to the boil, then reduce the heat and simmer for a further 5 minutes.

3 Transfer the fennel mixture to the slow cooker. Put the fish on top and sprinkle with the dill seeds. Cover and cook on high for 1¼ –1½ hours, until the flesh flakes easily.

4 Carefully transfer the fish to warmed individual plates. Remove and discard the bay leaf. Spoon the fennel and some of the cooking juices over the fish and serve immediately with salad leaves.

sole & prawn cream

serves 4

- 900 g/2 lb potatoes, cut into chunks
- 700 g/1 lb 9 oz sole fillets
- 25 g/1 oz butter, plus extra for greasing
- 2 egg yolks
- 175 g/6 oz Cheddar cheese, grated
- 1 tbsp chopped fresh flat-leaf parsley, plus extra sprigs to garnish
- 550 g/1 lb 4 oz cooked peeled prawns
- salt and pepper

1 Put the potatoes into a saucepan, pour in water to cover, add a pinch of salt and bring to the boil. Reduce the heat, cover and cook for 20–25 minutes, until soft but not falling apart.

2 Meanwhile, grease a 1.2-litre/2-pint pudding basin with butter, then line it with the fish fillets, skin-side inwards and with the tail ends overlapping the rim. Cut out a double round of greaseproof paper that is 5 cm/2 inches wider than the rim of the basin. Grease one side with butter.

3 Drain the potatoes in a colander. Return to the pan, add the butter and reheat gently until it has melted. Remove from the heat and mash well, then stir in the egg yolks, cheese and chopped parsley. Season lightly with salt and pepper.

4 Make alternating layers of the mashed potato mixture and prawns in the pudding basin, then fold over the overlapping fish fillets. Cover the basin with the greaseproof paper rounds and tie in place with string. Stand the basin on a trivet in the slow cooker and pour in enough boiling water to come about halfway up the side. Cover and cook on low for 2½ hours.

5 Carefully remove the basin from the slow cooker and discard the greaseproof paper. Turn out onto a warmed serving dish. Garnish with parsley sprigs and serve immediately.

french-style fish stew

serves 4-6

- large pinch of saffron threads
- 1 prepared squid
- 900 g/2 lb mixed white fish, such as sea bass or monkfish, filleted and cut into large chunks
- 24 large raw prawns, peeled and deveined, heads and shells reserved
- 2 tbsp olive oil
- 1 large onion, finely chopped
- 1 fennel bulb, thinly sliced, feathery fronds reserved
- 2 large garlic cloves, crushed
- 4 tbsp Pernod
- 1 litre/1¾ pints fish stock
- 400 g/14 oz canned chopped tomatoes, drained
- 1 tbsp tomato purée
- 1 bay leaf
- pinch of sugar
- salt and pepper

1 Toast the saffron threads in a dry frying pan over a high heat, for 1 minute. Set aside. Cut off and reserve the tentacles from the squid and slice the body into 5-mm/¼ -inch rings. Place the seafood and fish in a bowl, cover and chill in the refrigerator until required. Tie the heads and shells of the prawns in a piece of muslin.

2 Heat the oil in a frying pan. Add the onion and fennel and cook over a low heat, for 5 minutes. Add the garlic and cook for 2 minutes. Remove the pan from the heat. Heat the Pernod in a saucepan, ignite and pour it over the onion and fennel, gently shaking the frying pan until the flames have died down.

3 Return the frying pan to the heat, stir in the toasted saffron, stock, tomatoes, tomato purée, bay leaf and sugar, and season with salt and pepper. Bring to the boil, then transfer to the slow cooker. Add the bag of prawn shells, cover and cook on low for 6 hours.

4 Remove and discard the bag of prawn shells and the bay leaf. Add the fish and seafood to the slow cooker, cover and cook on high for 30 minutes, until the fish flakes easily. Serve garnished with the reserved fennel fronds.

louisiana gumbo

serves 6

- 2 tbsp sunflower oil
- 175 g/6 oz okra, trimmed and cut into 2.5-cm/ 1-inch pieces
- 2 onions, finely chopped
- 4 celery sticks, very finely chopped
- 1 garlic clove, finely chopped
- 2 tbsp plain flour
- ½ tsp sugar
- 1 tsp ground cumin
- 700ml/1¼ pints fish stock
- 1 red pepper, deseeded and chopped
- 1 green pepper, deseeded and chopped
- 2 large tomatoes, chopped
- 4 tbsp chopped fresh parsley
- 1 tbsp chopped fresh coriander
- Tabasco sauce
- 350 g/12 oz large raw prawns, peeled and deveined
- 350 g/12 oz cod or haddock fillets, skinned and cut into 2.5-cm/1-inch chunks
- 350 g/12 oz monkfish fillet, cut into 2.5-cm/1-inch chunks
- salt and pepper

1 Heat half the oil in a heavy-based frying pan. Add the okra and cook over a low heat, stirring frequently, for 5 minutes until browned. Using a slotted spoon, transfer the okra to the slow cooker.

2 Add the remaining oil to the pan. Add the onions and celery and cook over a low heat, stirring occasionally, for 5 minutes until softened. Add the garlic and cook, stirring frequently, for 1 minute, then sprinkle in the flour, sugar and cumin, and season with salt and pepper. Cook, stirring constantly, for 2 minutes, then remove the pan from the heat.

3 Gradually stir in the stock, then return the pan to the heat and bring to the boil, stirring constantly. Pour the mixture over the okra and stir in the peppers and tomatoes. Cover and cook on low for 5–6 hours.

4 Stir in the parsley, coriander and Tabasco to taste, then add the prawns, cod and monkfish. Cover and cook on high for 30 minutes, until the fish is cooked and the prawns have changed colour. Taste and adjust the seasoning if necessary and serve.

jambalaya

serves 4

- ½ tsp cayenne pepper
- 2 tsp chopped fresh thyme
- 350 g/12 oz skinless, boneless chicken breasts, diced
- 2 tbsp corn oil
- 2 onions, chopped
- 2 garlic cloves, finely chopped
- 2 green peppers, deseeded and chopped
- 2 celery sticks, chopped
- 115 g/4 oz smoked ham, chopped
- 175 g/6 oz chorizo sausage, sliced
- 400 g/14 oz canned chopped tomatoes
- 2 tbsp tomato purée
- 225 ml/8 fl oz chicken stock
- 450 g/1 lb raw prawns, peeled and deveined
- 450 g/1 lb cooked rice
- salt and pepper
- snipped fresh chives, to garnish

1 Mix the cayenne pepper, ½ teaspoon of pepper, 1 teaspoon of salt and the thyme together in a bowl. Add the chicken and toss to coat.

2 Heat the oil in a large heavy-based saucepan. Add the onions, garlic, green peppers and celery, and cook over a low heat, stirring occasionally, for 5 minutes. Add the chicken and cook over a medium heat, stirring frequently, for a further 5 minutes, until golden all over. Stir in the ham, chorizo, tomatoes, tomato purée and stock, and bring to the boil.

3 Transfer the mixture to the slow cooker. Cover and cook on low for 6 hours. Add the prawns and rice, re-cover and cook on high for 30 minutes.

4 Taste and adjust the seasoning, adding salt and pepper if necessary. Transfer to warmed plates, garnish with chives and serve immediately.

south-western seafood stew

serves 4

- 2 tbsp olive oil, plus extra for drizzling
- 1 large onion, chopped
- 4 garlic cloves, finely chopped
- 1 yellow pepper, deseeded and chopped
- 1 red pepper, deseeded and chopped
- 1 orange pepper, deseeded and chopped
- 450 g/1 lb tomatoes, peeled and chopped
- 2 large mild green chillies, such as poblano, chopped
- finely grated rind and juice of 1 lime
- 2 tbsp chopped fresh coriander, plus extra leaves to garnish
- 1 bay leaf
- 450 ml/16 fl oz fish, vegetable or chicken stock
- 450 g/1 lb red mullet fillets
- 450 g/1 lb raw prawns
- 225 g/8 oz prepared squid
- salt and pepper

1 Heat the oil in a saucepan. Add the onion and garlic, and cook over a low heat, stirring occasionally, for 5 minutes, until softened. Add the peppers, tomatoes and chillies, and cook, stirring frequently, for 5 minutes. Stir in the lime rind and juice, add the chopped coriander and bay leaf, and pour in the stock. Bring to the boil, stirring occasionally.

2 Transfer the mixture to the slow cooker, cover and cook on low for 7½ hours. Meanwhile, skin the fish fillets, if necessary, and cut the flesh into chunks. Peel and devein the prawns. Cut the squid bodies into rings and halve the tentacles or leave them whole.

3 Add the seafood to the stew, season to taste with salt and pepper, re-cover and cook on high for 30 minutes, or until tender and cooked through. Remove and discard the bay leaf. Transfer to warmed serving bowls, garnish with coriander leaves and serve immediately.

seafood in saffron sauce

serves 4

- 2 tbsp olive oil
- 1 onion, sliced
- 2 celery sticks, sliced
- pinch of saffron threads
- 1 tbsp chopped fresh thyme
- 2 garlic cloves, finely chopped
- 800 g/1 lb 12 oz canned chopped tomatoes, drained
- 175 ml/6 fl oz dry white wine
- 2 litres/3½ pints fish stock
- 225 g/8 oz live clams
- 225 g/8 oz live mussels
- 350 g/12 oz red mullet fillets
- 450 g/1 lb monkfish fillets
- 225 g/8 oz squid rings, thawed if frozen
- 2 tbsp shredded fresh basil leaves
- salt and pepper

1 Heat the oil in a heavy-based frying pan. Add the onion, celery, saffron, thyme and a pinch of salt, and cook over a low heat, stirring occasionally, for 5 minutes until softened. Add the garlic and cook, stirring constantly, for 2 minutes.

2 Add the tomatoes, wine and stock, season with salt and pepper, and bring to the boil, stirring constantly. Transfer the mixture to the slow cooker, cover and cook on low for 5 hours.

3 Meanwhile, scrub the shellfish under cold running water and pull the 'beards' off the mussels. Discard any with broken shells or that do not shut immediately when sharply tapped. Cut the mullet and monkfish fillets into bite-sized chunks.

4 Add the pieces of fish, the shellfish and the squid rings to the slow cooker, re-cover and cook on high for 30 minutes, until the clams and mussels have opened and the fish is cooked through. Discard any shellfish that remain closed. Stir in the basil and serve immediately.

vegetable paella

serves 6

- 4 tbsp olive oil
- 1 Spanish onion, sliced
- 2 garlic cloves, finely chopped
- 1 litre/1¾ pints hot vegetable stock
- large pinch of saffron threads, lightly crushed
- 1 yellow pepper, deseeded and sliced
- 1 red pepper, deseeded and sliced
- 1 large aubergine, diced
- 225 g/8 oz paella or risotto rice
- 450 g/1 lb tomatoes, peeled and chopped
- 115 g/4 oz chestnut mushrooms, sliced
- 115 g/4 oz French beans, halved
- 400 g/14 oz canned borlotti beans, drained and rinsed
- salt and pepper

1 Heat the oil in a large frying pan. Add the onion and garlic, and cook over a low heat, stirring occasionally, for 5 minutes, until softened. Put 3 tablespoons of the hot stock into a small bowl and stir in the saffron, then set aside to infuse.

2 Add the peppers and aubergine to the pan and cook, stirring occasionally, for 5 minutes. Add the rice and cook, stirring constantly, for 1 minute, until the grains are coated with oil and glistening. Pour in the remaining stock and add the tomatoes, mushrooms, French beans and borlotti beans. Stir in the saffron mixture and season to taste with salt and pepper.

3 Transfer the mixture to the slow cooker, cover and cook on low for 2½ –3 hours, until the rice is tender and the stock has been absorbed. Transfer to warmed serving plates and serve immediately.

Enjoy
delicious
desserts

chocolate cake

serves 8

- 375 g/13 oz plain dark chocolate
- 175 g/6 oz unsalted butter, plus extra for greasing
- 175 g/6 oz light muscovado sugar
- 4 eggs
- 2 tsp vanilla extract
- 150 g/5½ oz self-raising flour
- 55 g/2 oz ground almonds
- 125 ml/4 fl oz double cream
- icing sugar, for dusting

1 Place a trivet or a ring of crumpled foil in the base of the slow cooker. Grease and base-line a 20-cm/8-inch diameter, deep cake tin, or a tin that fits into your slow cooker.

2 Melt 250 g/9 oz of the chocolate in a bowl over a saucepan of hot water. Remove from the heat and cool slightly.

3 Beat the butter and sugar in a large bowl until pale and fluffy. Gradually beat in the eggs. Stir in the melted chocolate and 1 teaspoon of the vanilla extract. Fold in the flour and almonds evenly.

4 Spoon the mixture into the tin, spreading evenly. Place in the slow cooker, cover and cook on high for 2½ hours, or until risen and springy to the touch.

5 Remove from the slow cooker and leave the cake in the tin for 10 minutes. Turn out and cool on a wire rack.

6 Place the remaining chocolate and vanilla extract in a saucepan with the cream and heat gently, stirring, until melted. Cool until thick enough to spread. Split the cake into two layers and sandwich together with the filling. Dust with icing sugar and serve.

chocolate & walnut sponge

serves 4–6

- 55 g/2 oz cocoa powder, plus extra for dusting
- 2 tbsp milk
- 115 g/4 oz self-raising flour
- pinch of salt
- 115 g/4 oz unsalted butter, softened, plus extra for greasing
- 115 g/4 oz caster sugar
- 2 eggs, lightly beaten
- 55 g/2 oz walnut halves, chopped
- whipped cream, to serve

1 Grease a 1.2-litre/2-pint pudding basin with butter. Cut out a double round of greaseproof paper that is 7 cm/2¾ inches wider than the rim of the basin and grease one side with butter.

2 Mix the cocoa and the milk to a paste in a small bowl. Sift together the flour and salt into a separate small bowl. Set aside.

3 Beat together the butter and sugar in a large bowl until pale and fluffy. Gradually beat in the eggs, a little at a time, then gently fold in the sifted flour mixture, followed by the cocoa mixture and the walnuts.

4 Spoon the mixture into the prepared basin. Cover the basin with the greaseproof paper rounds, buttered-side down, and tie in place with string. Stand the basin on a trivet in the slow cooker and pour in enough boiling water to come about halfway up the side of the basin. Cover and cook on high for 3–3½ hours.

5 Carefully remove the basin from the slow cooker, and discard the greaseproof paper. Run a knife around the inside of the basin, then turn out onto a warmed serving dish. Serve immediately with whipped cream, dusted with cocoa.

hazelnut steamed sponge

serves 6

- 115 g/4 oz unsalted butter, plus extra for greasing
- 115 g/4 oz toasted hazelnuts, chopped
- 115 g/4 oz soft dark brown sugar
- 2 eggs, lightly beaten
- 115 g/4 oz self-raising flour
- 1 tbsp lemon juice

toffee sauce

- 55 g/2 oz unsalted butter
- 55 g/2 oz soft dark brown sugar
- 4 tbsp double cream
- 1 tbsp lemon juice

1 Grease an 850-ml/1½-pint pudding basin with butter and sprinkle half the nuts over the base. Cut two rounds of greaseproof paper, about 7 cm/2¾ inches wider than the rime of the basin.

2 To make the toffee sauce, put all of the ingredients into a saucepan. Cook over a very low heat, stirring continuously, until the mixture is smooth. Remove from the heat and pour half the sauce into the prepared basin. Swirl gently to coat the sides of the basin.

3 Beat together the butter and sugar in a bowl until light and fluffy. Gradually beat in the eggs, then gently fold in the flour, lemon juice and the remaining hazelnuts. Spoon the mixture into the basin. Cover the basin with the greaseproof paper rounds and tie in place with string. Stand the basin on a trivet in the slow cooker and pour in enough boiling water to come about halfway up the side of the basin. Cover and cook on high for 3–3¼ hours.

4 Before serving, reheat the remaining toffee sauce. Remove the basin from the slow cooker and discard the greaseproof paper. Run a knife around the inside of the basin, then turn out onto a warmed serving dish. Serve with the warm toffee sauce.

lemon sponge

serves 4

- 140 g/5 oz caster sugar
- 3 eggs, separated
- 300 ml/10 fl oz milk
- 3 tbsp self-raising flour, sifted
- 150 ml/5 fl oz lemon juice
- icing sugar, for dusting

1 Using an electric mixer, beat the caster sugar with the egg yolks in a bowl. Gradually beat in the milk, followed by the flour and the lemon juice.

2 Whisk the egg whites in a separate grease-free bowl until stiff. Fold half the whites into the yolk mixture using a plastic spatula in a figure-of-eight movement, then fold in the remainder. Try not to knock out the air.

3 Pour the mixture into a heatproof dish and cover with foil. Stand the dish on a trivet in the slow cooker and pour in enough boiling water to come about one third of the way up the side of the dish. Cover and cook on high for 2½ hours, until the mixture has set and the sauce and sponge have separated.

4 Carefully remove the dish from the slow cooker and discard the foil. Transfer to warmed bowls, lightly dust with icing sugar and serve immediately.

strawberry cheesecake

serves 6–8

- 85 g/3 oz unsalted butter, melted
- 140 g/5 oz digestive biscuits, crushed
- 300 g/10½ oz strawberries
- 600 g/1 lb 5 oz full-fat soft cheese
- 225 g/8 oz caster sugar
- 2 large eggs, beaten
- 2 tbsp cornflour
- finely grated rind and juice of 1 lemon

1 Place a trivet or a ring of crumpled foil in the base of the slow cooker. Stir the butter into the crushed biscuits and press into the base of a 20-cm/8-inch round springform tin, or a tin that fits into your slow cooker.

2 Purée or mash half the strawberries and whisk together with the cheese, sugar, eggs, cornflour and lemon rind and juice until smooth.

3 Tip the mixture into the tin and place in the slow cooker. Cover and cook on high for about 2 hours or until almost set.

4 Turn off the slow cooker and leave the cheesecake in the cooker for 2 hours. Remove and cool completely, then carefully turn out of the tin.

5 Decorate with the remaining strawberries and serve.

apple crumble

serves 4

- 55 g/2 oz plain flour
- 55 g/2 oz rolled oats
- 150 g/5½ oz light muscovado sugar
- ½ tsp freshly grated nutmeg
- ½ tsp ground cinnamon
- 115 g/4 oz unsalted butter, softened
- 4 cooking apples, peeled, cored and sliced
- 4–5 tbsp apple juice
- Greek yogurt, to serve

1 Sift the flour into a bowl and stir in the oats, sugar, nutmeg and cinnamon. Add the butter and mix in with a pastry blender or the tines of a fork.

2 Place the apple slices in the base of the slow cooker and add the apple juice. Sprinkle the flour mixture evenly over them.

3 Cover and cook on low for 5½ hours. Serve hot, warm or cold with yogurt.

rice pudding

serves 4

- 140 g/5 oz short-grain rice
- 1 litre/1¾ pints milk
- 115 g/4 oz granulated sugar
- 1 tsp vanilla extract
- ground cinnamon,
  to decorate

1 Rinse the rice well under cold running water and drain thoroughly. Pour the milk into a large heavy-based saucepan, add the sugar and bring to the boil, stirring constantly. Sprinkle in the rice, stir well and simmer gently for 10–15 minutes. Transfer the mixture to a heatproof dish and cover with foil.

2 Stand the dish on a trivet in the slow cooker and pour in enough boiling water to come about one third of the way up the side of the dish. Cover and cook on high for 2 hours.

3 Remove the dish from the slow cooker and discard the foil. Stir the vanilla extract into the rice, then spoon it into warmed bowls. Lightly dust with cinnamon and serve immediately.

italian bread pudding

serves 6

- unsalted butter, for greasing
- 6 slices panettone
- 3 tbsp Marsala
- 300 ml/10 fl oz milk
- 300 ml/10 fl oz single cream
- 100 g/3½ oz caster sugar
- grated rind of ½ lemon
- pinch of ground cinnamon
- 3 large eggs, lightly beaten

1 Grease a 1-litre/1¾ -pint pudding basin with butter. Place the panettone on a deep plate and sprinkle with the Marsala.

2 Pour the milk and cream into a saucepan and add the sugar, lemon rind and cinnamon. Gradually bring to the boil over a low heat, stirring until the sugar has dissolved. Remove the pan from the heat and leave to cool slightly, then pour the mixture onto the eggs, beating constantly.

3 Place the panettone in the prepared basin, pour in the egg mixture and cover with foil. Stand the basin on a trivet in the slow cooker and pour in enough boiling water to come about one third of the way up the side of the basin. Cover and cook on high for 2½ hours, until set.

4 Carefully remove the basin from the slow cooker and discard the foil. Leave to cool, then chill in the refrigerator until required. Run a knife around the inside of the basin, then turn out onto a serving dish. Serve immediately.

thai black rice pudding

serves 4
- 175 g/6 oz black glutinous rice
- 2 tbsp soft light brown sugar
- 450 ml/16 fl oz canned coconut milk
- 225 ml/8 fl oz water
- 3 eggs
- 2 tbsp caster sugar

1 Mix the rice, brown sugar and half the coconut milk together in a saucepan, then stir in the water. Bring to the boil, then reduce the heat and simmer, stirring occasionally, for 15 minutes, until almost all the liquid has been absorbed. Transfer the mixture to a heatproof dish or individual ramekins.

2 Lightly beat the eggs with the remaining coconut milk and the caster sugar. Strain, then pour the mixture over the rice.

3 Cover the dish with foil. Stand the dish on a trivet in the slow cooker and pour in enough boiling water to come about one third of the way up the side of the dish. Cover and cook on high for 2–2½ hours, until set. Carefully remove the dish from the slow cooker and discard the foil. Serve hot or cold.

poached peaches in marsala

serves 4-6

- 150 ml/5 fl oz Marsala
- 175 ml/6 fl oz water
- 4 tbsp caster sugar
- 1 vanilla pod,
  split lengthways
- 6 peaches, cut into wedges
  and stoned
- 2 tsp cornflour
- crème fraîche or Greek
  yogurt, to serve

1 Pour the Marsala and 150 ml/5 fl oz of the water into a saucepan and add the sugar and vanilla pod. Set the pan over a low heat and stir until the sugar has dissolved, then bring to the boil without stirring. Remove from the heat.

2 Put the peaches into the slow cooker and pour the syrup over them. Cover and cook on high for 1–1½ hours, until the fruit is tender.

3 Using a slotted spoon, gently transfer the peaches to a serving dish. Remove the vanilla pod from the slow cooker and scrape the seeds into the syrup with the point of a knife. Discard the pod. Stir the cornflour to a paste with the remaining water in a small bowl, then stir into the syrup. Re-cover and cook on high for 15 minutes, stirring occasionally.

4 Spoon the syrup over the fruit and leave to cool slightly. Serve warm or chill in the refrigerator for 2 hours before serving with crème fraîche or yogurt.

blushing pears

serves 6

- 6 small ripe pears
- 225 ml/8 fl oz ruby port
- 200 g/7 oz caster sugar
- 1 tsp finely chopped crystallized ginger
- 2 tbsp lemon juice
- whipped cream or Greek yogurt, to serve

1 Peel the pears, cut them in half lengthways and scoop out the cores. Place them in the slow cooker.

2 Combine the port, sugar, ginger and lemon juice in a jug and pour the mixture over the pears. Cover and cook on low for 4 hours, until the pears are tender.

3 Leave the pears to cool in the slow cooker, then carefully transfer to a bowl and chill in the refrigerator until required.

4 To serve, cut each pear half into about six slices lengthways, leaving the fruit intact at the stalk end. Carefully lift the pear halves onto serving plates and press gently to fan out the slices. Spoon the cooking juices over the pears and serve immediately with cream.

almond charlotte

serves 4
- unsalted butter, for greasing
- 10–12 sponge fingers
- 300 ml/10 fl oz milk
- 2 eggs
- 2 tbsp caster sugar
- 55 g/2 oz blanched almonds, chopped
- 4–5 drops almond extract

sherry sauce
- 1 tbsp caster sugar
- 3 egg yolks
- 150 ml/5 fl oz cream sherry

1 Grease a 600-ml/1-pint pudding basin with butter. Line the basin with the sponge fingers, cutting them to fit and placing them cut-sides down and sugar-coated sides outwards. Cover the base of the basin with some of the offcuts.

2 Pour the milk into a saucepan and bring just to the boil, then remove from the heat. Beat together the eggs and sugar in a heatproof bowl until combined, then stir in the milk. Stir in the almonds and almond extract.

3 Carefully pour the mixture into the prepared basin, making sure that the sponge fingers stay in place, and cover with foil. Stand the basin on a trivet in the slow cooker and pour in enough boiling water to come about halfway up the side of the dish. Cover and cook on high for 3–3½ hours, until set.

4 Shortly before serving, make the sherry sauce. Put the sugar, egg yolks and sherry into a heatproof bowl. Set the bowl over a saucepan of simmering water, without allowing the bottom of the bowl to touch the surface of the water. Whisk well until the mixture thickens, but do not allow it to boil. Remove from the heat.

5 Carefully remove the basin from the slow cooker and discard the foil. Leave to stand for 2–3 minutes, then turn out onto a warmed serving plate. Pour the sherry sauce around it and serve immediately.

crème brûlée

serves 6

- 1 vanilla pod
- 1 litre/1¾ pints double cream
- 6 egg yolks
- 100 g/3½ oz caster sugar
- 85 g/3 oz soft light brown sugar

1 Using a sharp knife, split the vanilla pod in half lengthways, scrape the seeds into a saucepan and add the pod. Pour in the cream and bring just to the boil, stirring constantly. Remove from the heat, cover and leave to infuse for 20 minutes.

2 Whisk together the egg yolks and caster sugar in a bowl until thoroughly mixed. Remove and discard the vanilla pod from the pan, then whisk the cream into the egg yolk mixture. Strain the mixture into a large jug.

3 Divide the mixture between six ramekins and cover each with foil. Stand the ramekins on a trivet in the slow cooker and pour in enough boiling water to come about halfway up the sides of the ramekins. Cover and cook on low for 3–3½ hours, until just set. Remove the slow cooker pot from the base and leave to cool completely, then remove the ramekins and chill in the refrigerator for at least 4 hours.

4 Preheat the grill. Sprinkle the brown sugar evenly over the surface of each dessert, then cook under the preheated grill for 30–60 seconds, until the sugar has melted and caramelized. Alternatively, you can use a cook's blowtorch. Return the ramekins to the refrigerator and chill for a further hour before serving.

chocolate pots

serves 6
- 300 ml/10 fl oz single cream
- 300 ml/10 fl oz milk
- 225 g/8 oz plain chocolate, broken into small pieces
- 1 large egg
- 4 egg yolks
- 4 tbsp caster sugar
- 150 ml/5 fl oz double cream
- chocolate curls, to decorate

1 Pour the single cream and milk into a saucepan and add the chocolate. Set the pan over a very low heat and stir until the chocolate has melted and the mixture is smooth. Remove from the heat and leave to cool for 10 minutes.

2 Beat together the egg, egg yolks and sugar in a bowl until combined. Gradually stir in the chocolate mixture until thoroughly blended, then strain into a jug.

3 Divide the mixture between six ramekins and cover each with foil. Stand the ramekins on a trivet in the slow cooker and pour in enough boiling water to come about halfway up the sides of the ramekins. Cover and cook on low for 3–3½ hours, until just set. Remove the slow cooker pot from the base and leave to cool completely, then remove the ramekins and chill in the refrigerator for at least 4 hours.

4 Whip the double cream in a bowl until it holds soft peaks. Top each chocolate pot with a little of the whipped cream and decorate with chocolate curls. Serve immediately.

Index